500
appetizers

500 appetizers

the only appetizer compendium you'll ever need

Susannah Blake

SELLERS

PUBLISHING

A Quintet Book

Published by Sellers Publishing Inc.
161 John Roberts Road, South Portland, Maine 04106
For ordering information:
(800) 625-3386 Toll Free
(207) 772-6814 Fax
Visit our Web site: www.rsvp.com • E-mail: rsp@rsvp.com

President and Publisher: Ronnie Sellers
Publishing Director: Robin Haywood
Managing Editor Mary Baldwin

ISBN-13: 978-1-56906-976-9
QUIN.LCOC

This book was designed and produced by
Quintet Publishing Limited
6 Blundell Street
London N7 9BH

Library of Congress Control Number: 2006935718

Senior Editor: Ruth Patrick
Editors: Jodie Gaudet, Bridget Jones
Art Director: Dean Martin
Photography: Ian Garlick
Designer: Janis Utton
Home Economist: Wendy Sweetser
Creative Director: Richard Dewing
Publisher: Gaynor Sermon

10 9 8 7 6 5 4 3 2

Manufactured in Singapore by Pica Digital Pte Ltd.
Printed in China by SNP Leefung Printers Ltd.

contents

introduction

Appetizers can be wonderfully varied and yet they all do exactly what their title suggests — whet the appetite and stimulate the tastebuds. Whether it's the simplest bowl of salted nuts to nibble with pre-dinner drinks, elegant cocktail canapés to accompany sophisticated aperitifs, or a stunning starter to savor at the table, they all share the same function. They should make the mouth water, encourage guests to relax, and help to create a convivial atmosphere. They are also there to stave off possible hunger pangs until the main event, but be aware that appetizers should never spoil the appetite. Instead, they should tease it lightly by offering a stimulating foretaste of the culinary delights to come.

international appetizers

All over the world, countless bite-size morsels are served as appetizers. Some are traditionally offered as snacks between meals but work perfectly in the pre-meal role, while others have always been served as little taste-tempters. From France come the tiniest of appetizers — *amuse bouches* — miniature mouthfuls that play with everyone's tastebuds even before the first course arrives. Usually beautifully presented, these morsels range from mini crostini to a spoonful of soup to flirt with your appetite.

Also from France there are the classic hors d'oeuvres, traditionally a selection of small portions — usually cold — served at the beginning of a meal. Hors d'oeuvres may include anything from charcuterie and salad vegetables to smoked fish, anchovies, and olives presented on a single platter or board. The Italians have a similar first-course tradition known as antipasti, literally meaning "before pasta." They can include the simplest bruschetta with garlic and olive oil, or a whole array of delicious savories, such as crisp golden polenta; crostini topped with creamy mushrooms; marinated charbroiled vegetables; a simple mozzarella, tomato, and basil salad; stuffed baked mussels; and wafer-thin slices of delicate prosciutto.

Russians enjoy zakusi, literally meaning "little bites" and originally referring to sweet delicacies served after a meal, but now describing savories served before the meal, often with vodka. They may include salted and pickled fish, caviar, sausage, preserved meats, pickled cucumbers, rye bread, and little hot pastries.

From Spain and the Middle East come tapas and meze — perfect for serving as appetizers as well as, in the traditional style, little snacks to accompany drinks. In Spain, tapas are served in bars. Sometimes they arrive automatically with each drink, while in other bars you need to order them. Often salty (olives, anchovies, or little rounds of spicy grilled chorizo), not only are they perfect with a glass of sherry or a cold beer, but they also encourage the customer to sip their drink. The range of tapas is enormous and varies from the classic spicy fried potatoes (*patatas bravas*) to wedges of tortilla, simple salads, and wonderful seafood.

In contrast, meze are usually served in the home, as an array of snacks to offer guests. The word *meze* comes from the Persian *maz*, meaning "taste" or "relish." The tradition spread from Turkey into Greece, Lebanon, and throughout north Africa. Typically, meze range from the simplest bowl of olives or cubes of cheese to dips such as taramasalata, tsatsiki, and hummus, salads such as tabbouleh, and more substantial snacks such as falafel and pastries. Just one or a selection may be served for guests to nibble on.

Asia also produces an inspired array of traditional snacks. Japanese sushi, stunningly presented, appeals to the eye and the palate, and the small portions are perfect for popping into your mouth as you chat over drinks. Similarly, Chinese dim sum are the ideal dishes to get the digestive juices flowing. Traditionally, dim sum are served in tea houses, and you would no more consider going to a tea house without ordering a few little morsels than going to a tapas bar and not ordering something to nibble on. There are, finally, those classic street-foods, the snacks sold on street corners all over Asia — from Indian samosas and pakoras to Thai fishcakes, Indonesian satay, and Vietnamese salt-and-pepper squid.

equipment

Depending on the appetizer, you rarely need any special equipment other than the usual kitchen kit — a good, sharp chopping knife, cutting board, mixing bowls and spoons, measuring spoons, cups, scales, a baking sheet and pans, wire rack, and food processor or blender. Only a few appetizers, such as sushi, will require specialist equipment (a sushi mat for rolling up classic sushi rolls). Serving is important — beautiful presentation has as much to do with making the mouth water as the aroma of the food.

serving bowls and platters
These are particularly important for canapés, cocktail snacks, and dips and dippers.
• Flat platters are perfect for serving tartlets, pizza squares, and skewered foods.
• A large dish or shallow bowl big enough to hold a smaller bowl is just right for serving both dips and dippers.
• Smaller bowls are ideal for olives, nuts, and cocktail crackers.

individual plates and bowls
For appetizers enjoyed at the table, such as salads and tarts, placing them on individual plates adds a special style. A salad arranged on a small plate or in an individual bowl usually looks far more appealing than one served in a large dish, to be spooned out at the table.

For tapas or meze, where several small dishes are served at once, you will need several small serving dishes as well as individual plates for guests to pile with the array of morsels.

skewers, picks, and sticks
These are essential for satay or kebabs, but are also good for skewering "messy" or awkward foods, such as salt-and-pepper squid or marinated olives. Many kinds of skewers are available, from the simplest bamboo type to metal skewers with decorative handles.

The simplest picks, sticks, and spikes for selecting pieces of food are cocktail sticks or toothpicks — the attractive ones transform simple ingredients offered with drinks into something of an elegant appetizer.

napkins

Napkins are essential for cleaning sticky or greasy fingers, or for holding larger snacks that provide two or three mouthfuls before they are finished. A pizza square or golden chicken wing is much easier to handle when you have a napkin to rest it on as you chat between mouthfuls. Paper napkins are entirely acceptable for appetizers served with drinks, but for a more formal course at the table, you may prefer to go for linen.

debris dishes

Foods that leave guests clutching redundant parts, such as an olive pit, a skewer, or a chicken bone, should always be shadowed by a few strategically placed vessels to accommodate these unwanted leftovers. These foods are there to help get a party going and smooth the way for social chit-chat — so don't make your guests wonder how to discard their nibble-sticks without committing a terrible social faux pas!

gorgeous garnishes

The garnish adds visual appeal and should also be aromatic and flavorsome. Fresh herbs are a great standby, whether sprinkled over soups, on canapés or meze. Snipped chives, a sprig of oregano or a fragrant leaf, a wafer-thin slice of cucumber or half a cherry tomato, a twist of lemon or smoked salmon, or a dab of caviar can be the finishing touch that turns a lovely canapé into a simply stunning one. If the appetizers are prepared in advance, you can top, drizzle, or sprinkle in a matter of seconds and serve appetizers that look utterly irresistible.

making perfect appetizers

There are a few tricks for producing perfect appetizers. The main one is choosing the right appetizer for the right occasion. Are you throwing an elegant dinner party and want to impress your guests? Or is it a more casual affair for which a laid-back, anything-goes style is more suitable? Have you invited an intrepid crowd who'll try anything once? Or does your guest list include elderly relatives who would prefer to eat something they know and love, rather than try something new and exotic? Are you entertaining a crowd of ravenous teenagers who'll eat anything and everything in sight? Whoever you're entertaining, this book is packed with fun, delicious ideas that will suit any and every occasion.

For a fairly formal affair, dip into the chapters on mouthwatering salads and elegant starters. Each recipe tastes delicious, looks stunning, and is guaranteed to impress even the most discerning diners. For a casual occasion, why not try simple dips, chips, and sticks — they're great with drinks or for an informal party. For a taste of the exotic, nothing beats a plateful of meze or platter of Asian-style snacks. Those with more conventional taste will find little more enjoyable than simple chips and dips, or a light salad of fresh leaves.

getting the timing right

Good timing is another key feature of the perfect appetizer. Who wants to slave away in the kitchen while the guests are having fun? Choose appetizers that suit you, the cook. If you're serving at the kitchen table, chatting while cooking can be fun, but if you're entertaining elsewhere, go for dishes that can be prepared ahead or assembled at the last minute.

Most dips can be stored in the fridge, with just a quick stir before serving, and skewers can be left to marinate until it is time to grill. Salads can be combined and dressed just before serving. Many prepared toppings and bases can be assembled at the last minute.

It is also paramount to remember that an appetizer is just one course and that there is more to follow. So choosing an impressive, yet hassle-free, appetizer means you can

concentrate on getting the main course and dessert just right, knowing that the appetizer will keep everyone happy while you stay cool, calm, and collected.

dressing up and dressing down

Perfect presentation is key. The great thing about presentation is that you can dress dishes up or down to suit the occasion. A big basket of chicken wings simply placed on the table for the family to dig into is the ultimate relaxing, low-maintenance appetizer. Conversely, toss a bag of salad with a simple dressing, arrange it on plates, and nestle a few chicken wings on top, and an altogether more impressive appetizer evolves with minimum effort.

Many of the recipes in this book can be dressed up or down according to the occasion. Nestle three or four canapés on each plate with a few spinach leaves, add a drizzle of oil, and suddenly you have an elegant starter rather than a pre-dinner nibble. Meze, tapas, and Asian bites can all be treated in this way. A simple salad with chicken satay accompanied by a tiny individual pot of satay sauce provides an entirely different type of appetizer from a platter of satay with a big bowl of peanut sauce, passed around as everyone sips aperitifs.

Meze, tapas, or Asian snacks are also the perfect choice if you fancy an exotic feast of dishes from around the world. Why not start with a selection of meze before moving on to a main course of a Moroccan tagine with couscous and a simple dessert of rosewater ice cream? Alternatively, nibble on a few tapas tasters before serving up a fabulous seafood paella, followed by the classic Spanish dessert crema catalana. Asian street food snacks are the ultimate dress-up/dress-down appetizers — as good served with drinks and a simple dip as plated up with drizzled sauces and a simple cucumber salad or red onion relish.

Dips are fantastically versatile too. Choose any of the dips in this book, just dollop some onto squares of pumpernickel or mini blinis, sprinkle with fresh herbs and . . . *voila*, suddenly you have a plate of stunning canapés, perfect for the most sophisticated of drinks parties.

The trick is to have fun. Use creative flair to transform your no-hassle, favorite savory dishes to suit any occasion.

instant appetizers

As well as working from the recipes, you can choose from a fabulous array of instant appetizers to conjure up at a moment's notice. With almost no effort, you'll be in the ultimate-host category!

quick dips

Supermarkets sell a range of fabulous ready-made dips, from fresh salsas to creamy classics and simple favorites, such as guacamole, taramasalata, and hummus. Just buy a tub, scoop it into a bowl and serve with some dippers, and your work is done.

If you want to make super-speedy dips of your own, go for a simple base, such as a good-quality mayonnaise, crème fraîche, sour cream, or plain yogurt. Stir in chopped fresh herbs, lemon zest, a spoonful or two of pesto, or a little crumbled blue cheese to make a simple dip. Other good additions include a splash or two of Tabasco sauce, finely chopped spring onions, capers, crushed anchovies, or garlic.

easy dippers

Every dip needs tasty dippers. Purchased savory snacks can be good on their own or used for dunking. Open the bag when guests arrive, tip them into a bowl, and serve. What could be simpler? Look for artisan crisps that come in a great choice of interesting flavors — guests are sure to be impressed that you've searched out special snacks rather than the usual supermarket fare.

Other fuss-free dippers include fingers of pita bread, either plain or lightly toasted. Crisp Italian breadsticks are another good choice for kids and adults alike. Tortilla chips and mini poppadoms are great for scooping, whether it's a Mexican-style salsa or a fragrant Indian relish; they're great for topping too. Depending on the occasion, turn them into bites with sophisticated toppings or simple munchies.

Raw vegetable sticks are ideal for dipping and dunking, and they make a refreshing, healthy choice. Carrots should be topped, tailed, and peeled, then cut into bite-size sticks. Cucumbers should be washed, seeded and cut into sticks. Bell peppers should be seeded, the cores removed, then sliced into sticks. Broccoli and cauliflower florets and cherry tomatoes also work. If you need to prepare vegetable sticks some time in advance, place them in a bowl and cover with plastic wrap to avoid them drying out, then store in the fridge until needed.

minute munchies

Nibbles to go with drinks are available at a moment's notice. A dish of olives or some marinated anchovies from the deli counter, a bag of honey-roasted nuts or a plate full of exotic cheese crackers is all you need. Buy a jar of stuffed grape leaves, arrange them on a platter, and simply squeeze lime juice over — delicious! Remember, it's all in the presentation.

shortcuts to canapés

Canapés are traditionally presented on some kind of bread base. Although you can make your own from scratch, you can take shortcuts and still end up with stunning appetizers.

• Ready-made blinis are available from most larger supermarkets, ready to be heated up in the oven for a few minutes.

• Pumpernickel bread makes a great base. Cut it into squares or use a cookie cutter to cut it into bite-size rounds. Then add the topping of your choice. You can use this technique on toasted bread as well. The result looks stunning but takes no effort at all.

• Flour tortillas make another fuss-free base. Smear them with a thin layer of filling, such as cream cheese, and add smoked salmon. Then roll them up tightly and slice the roll, using a serrated knife to make a plateful of mini pinwheels. Alternatively, cut the tortillas in half or into quarters and roll the pieces into mini cones ready to hold the filling of your choice.

fuss-free ingredients

As well as tricks and tips for making instant appetizers, there are also a number of ingredients that can take all the hassle out of preparation, which is just what you need when there are two more courses to prepare!

• Charbroiled or roasted vegetables are available bottled in olive oil. They taste great and are a time-saver for first courses. Wedges of artichokes and twists of roasted bell pepper look great on canapés or tossed into salads. Look out for Italian antipasti too — the vegetables are often bottled in a flavorful marinade that will really add a twist to a plain starter.

• Capers taste great and look more exotic than your average garnish when popped on top of a canapé or scattered on salad.

• Don't worry about cutting up your own crudités: buy a ready-prepared bag.

• To make polenta crostini, buy a block of ready-made polenta, then simply slice, brush with oil, and grill or fry until crisp before topping.

• Chickpeas and other legumes are great for wholesome dips. Don't soak and boil for hours but buy them canned instead, then drain them, throw them into the food processor with the chosen flavorings, purée for a moment, and you've got a delicious dip!

• Ready-rolled pastry is another boon for the busy cook. Simply take it out of the packet, cut into the required shapes, add toppings, and bake. What could be easier?

• Ready-made pizza crusts, like ready-rolled pastry, are also a great time-saver.

• Mini pita breads can be turned into instant pizza: top with pizza sauce and cheese, and bake for 10 minutes until golden.

• Indian naan bread can be transformed into hearty pizza ovals, then cut into wedges for the hungry masses.

• For salads, buy ready-prepared lettuce. There are lots of inspired combinations and it is so much easier than trying to create your own. The average bag is the perfect size for four appetizers, just right for most of the recipes in this book.

chips & sticks

These easy nibbles are crisp and satisfying — sure to please even the youngest party guest. Serve them on their own, buy a tub of ready-made dip, or pair them with one of the delicious dips in the next chapter. What could be simpler?

walnut & sun-dried tomato biscotti

see variations page 38

Based on the classic twice-baked Italian biscuit, these savory bites are a great alternative to a bag of chips. Their long, thin shape also makes them perfect for dunking into dips.

1/4 cup (1/2 stick) butter, at room temperature
2 eggs, lightly beaten
1 cup self-rising flour
1/4 cup cornmeal

2 oz. (about 10) sun-dried tomatoes in oil, drained and chopped
1/2 cup (3 1/2 oz.) walnuts, chopped

Preheat the oven to 350°F (180°C) and lightly grease and flour two baking sheets.

Beat the butter until smooth and creamy, then gradually beat in the eggs a little at a time. Sift the flour and cornmeal over the butter mixture and fold in using a metal spoon. Then stir in the sun-dried tomatoes and walnuts.

Divide the mixture between the baking sheets, shaping each portion into a flat loaf about 7 x 3 inches. Bake the loaves for about 20 minutes until pale golden. Transfer to a board.

Using a serrated knife, gently cut into 1/2-inch-thick slices. Arrange slices on baking sheets and cook for a further 10 minutes, until crisp and golden. Transfer to a wire rack to cool.

Makes about 24

parmesan tuiles

see variations page 39

These melt-in-the-mouth wafers are ridiculously easy to make and great for munching or dunking in a smooth dip. They can be stored in an airtight container for several days.

1 1/3 cups fresh Parmesan cheese, grated

Preheat the oven to 400°F (200°C). Line two baking sheets with nonstick parchment paper.

Spoon small mounds of cheese spaced well apart on the baking sheets and flatten them into rounds using the back of the spoon.

Bake the Parmesan for about 5 minutes, until golden. Leave on the baking sheets for a minute or so, to firm up. Use a palette knife to remove the tuiles carefully from the paper, and curl them over a rolling pin until set. Allow to cool completely on a wire rack.

Makes about 10

mozzarella &
basil quesadilla wedges

see variations page 40

Serve these melting Mexican wedges on their own or pair them with a tangy, zingy salsa for dipping.

Olive oil, for brushing
2 soft flour tortillas
5 oz. mozzarella cheese, thinly sliced

Dried chili flakes, for sprinkling
Handful of fresh basil leaves

Brush a large, nonstick frying pan with olive oil and heat it on medium heat. Lay 1 tortilla in the pan and arrange the cheese on top. Sprinkle with a good pinch or two of chili flakes and the basil leaves. Lay the second tortilla on top.

Cook for 1 to 2 minutes, until the tortilla is crisp and golden underneath. Then carefully flip it over and cook for a further 1 to 2 minutes, until crisp and golden on the second side.

Slide out onto a board, cut it into 12 wedges, and serve immediately.

Makes 12

poppy seed grissini

see variations page 41

These crunchy Italian breadsticks are delicious eaten as they are or served with a tangy dip. If you're feeling adventurous, try making a few different varieties to serve together.

1 3/4 cups white bread flour
1 tsp. dried yeast
1/2 tsp. salt

1 tbsp. olive oil
1/2 cup warm water
2 tsp. poppy seeds

Combine the flour, yeast, and salt in a large bowl and make a well in the middle. Pour in the oil and water and mix until a soft dough forms.

Turn out the dough onto a lightly floured surface and knead it for 5 to 10 minutes, until it is smooth and elastic. Place the dough in a large, clean, oiled bowl, cover with oiled plastic wrap, and leave to rise in a warm place for about 1 hour or until doubled in size.

Preheat the oven to 400°F (200°C) and lightly grease two baking sheets. Roll out the dough on a lightly floured surface into a 6 x 12 inch rectangle and cut into 1/2-inch-wide strips. Lightly roll the strips and arrange on the baking sheet, spacing them well apart.

Brush the grissini with water, sprinkle with poppy seeds, and bake for 10 to 12 minutes, until golden. Transfer to a wire rack to cool.

Makes about 24

herbed garlic pita toasts

see variations page 42

Serve these crispy, crunchy fingers of pita on their own or with a creamy dip. You can use white or whole wheat pita bread.

2 tbsp. olive oil
1 garlic clove, crushed
Ground black pepper

2 loaves pita bread
1 tbsp. chopped fresh parsley

In a small bowl, combine the oil and garlic and season with black pepper. Preheat the broiler.

Cut the pita breads in half horizontally, then carefully split them open. Slice each piece into three fingers. Arrange the pita fingers on the broiling rack and toast on one side for 1 to 2 minutes, until crisp and golden.

Turn the pita fingers, drizzle with the garlic oil, and broil for a further minute or so, until crisp and golden on the second side. Sprinkle with parsley and serve immediately.

Serves 4

simple rice noodle crisps

see variations page 43

Lacy rice noodle crisps make a stunning pre-dinner snack — perfect for whetting the appetite before an Asian-style meal. Serve them solo or with sweet chili sauce for dipping.

4 oz. rice vermicelli
1 red chili pepper, seeded and finely chopped
1 tsp. ground cumin

1 shallot, finely chopped
Salt
Vegetable oil, for deep-frying

Break the noodles into a large heatproof bowl and pour boiling water over to cover. Leave to stand for about 5 minutes, until softened.

Drain the noodles well and return them to the bowl. Sprinkle the chili, cumin, and shallot over the noodles, season with salt, and toss.

Heat about 2 inches oil to 375°F (190°C) in a wok, or until a cube of bread turns golden in about 1 minute.

Working in batches, drop tablespoonfuls of the noodles into the wok, pressing them flat using the back of a slotted spoon. Cook for about 2 minutes until crisp and golden, then lift out and drain on paper towels. Serve immediately.

Makes about 24

chili cheese straws

see variations page 44

Choose a really good, strongly flavored cheese for these crisp little twists. They have a wonderful bite of chili and will have your guests begging for more.

1 cup all-purpose flour
6 tbsp. (3/4 stick) butter, chilled and diced
3/4 cup mature cheddar cheese, grated
1/2 tsp. dried chili flakes

1 tsp. Worcestershire sauce
Paprika, for sprinkling (optional)

Blend the flour and butter in a food processor until the mixture resembles fine breadcrumbs. Add the cheese, chili, and Worcestershire sauce and process to make a soft dough.

Press the dough into a ball, wrap it in plastic wrap, and chill for about 15 minutes, until it has firmed up slightly. Preheat the oven to 325°F (170°C).

Roll out the dough on a lightly floured surface to about 1/4 inch thick, then cut it into strips measuring about 1/4 inch wide and 3 1/2 inches long. Twist the strips and lay them on a baking sheet.

Bake the twists for 10 to 15 minutes, until crisp and golden. Transfer them to a wire rack to cool. Sprinkle with paprika, if desired, before serving.

Makes about 30

anchovy crackers

see variations page 45

These peppery, salty bites are perfect with pre-dinner drinks. They are intriguingly delicious and difficult to resist.

1/2 cup all-purpose flour
1/4 cup (1/2 stick) butter, chilled and diced
1/3 cup freshly grated Parmesan cheese

4 anchovies in oil, drained
1/4 to 1/2 tsp. ground black pepper

Process the flour, butter, Parmesan, anchovies, and pepper in a food processor until the mixture comes together into a soft dough. Press the dough into a ball, wrap it in plastic wrap, and chill for about 15 minutes until it has firmed up slightly.

Meanwhile, preheat the oven to 400°F (200°C) and lightly grease two baking sheets.

Roll out the dough on a lightly floured surface to about 1/4 inch thick and cut into rounds using a 1 1/4-inch cookie cutter. Press the dough trimmings together and re-roll to make more rounds.

Arrange the rounds on the baking sheets and bake for about 6 minutes, until golden. Transfer the crackers to a wire rack to cool.

Makes about 40

beet crisps

see variations page 46

Colorful crisps made from wafer-thin slices of beet are easy to make and are great with drinks. Serve them on their own or with a little bowl of creamy dip.

1–2 fresh beets
Sunflower oil, for deep-frying

Coarse sea salt, for sprinkling

Trim and peel the beets, then use a mandolin or vegetable peeler to slice them into thin shavings. Rinse well, then pat dry with paper towels.

Pour enough sunflower oil into a pan to fill it about one-third full and heat to 375°F (190°C), or until a cube of bread turns golden in about 1 minute.

Working in batches, deep-fry the beet slices for about 1 minute, until crisp. Lift the beets out of the oil using a slotted spoon and drain them on a wire rack covered with several layers of paper towels. Sprinkle with salt and serve immediately.

Serves 4

tortilla chips

see variations page 47

Serve these crunchy golden chips on their own or Mexican-style with a spicy salsa or creamy guacamole.

2 soft flour tortillas   **Coarse sea salt, for sprinkling**
Vegetable oil, for deep-frying

Cut each tortilla into eight wedges. Pour oil into a deep frying pan until it is two-thirds full and heat to about 375°F (190°C), or until a cube of bread turns golden in about 1 minute.

Working in batches, add the tortilla wedges to the oil and fry for about 2 minutes, until golden. Remove from the oil using a slotted spoon and drain on paper towels. Sprinkle with salt and serve.

Serves 4

variations

walnut & sun-dried tomato biscotti

see base recipe page 19

walnut & cranberry biscotti
Prepare the basic recipe, adding 1/4 cup dried cranberries in place of the sun-dried tomatoes.

spicy sun-dried tomato & walnut biscotti
Prepare the basic recipe, adding 1/2 teaspoon crushed dried chili flakes with the tomatoes and walnuts.

pecan & olive biscotti
Prepare the basic recipe, using pecans in place of the walnuts and roughly chopped pitted olives in place of the sun-dried tomatoes.

almond, chili & date biscotti
Prepare the basic recipe, using almonds in place of the walnuts, and omitting the sun-dried tomatoes. Add 1/2 teaspoon dried chili flakes and 1/3 cup chopped pitted dried dates after folding in the flour.

variations

parmesan tuiles

see base recipe page 21

fennel & parmesan tuiles
Sprinkle about 1/8 teaspoon fennel seeds over the Parmesan before baking.

spicy cumin tuiles
Sprinkle a pinch or two of dried chili flakes and a pinch or two of ground cumin seeds over the Parmesan before baking.

parmesan tuiles with thyme
Sprinkle about 1/8 teaspoon fresh thyme leaves over the Parmesan before baking.

parmesan tuiles with sage
Sprinkle about 1/8 teaspoon chopped fresh sage over the Parmesan before baking.

variations

mozzarella & basil quesadilla wedges

see base recipe page 22

hot jalapeño quesadilla wedges
Prepare the basic quesadilla recipe, using 2 tablespoons sliced bottled jalapeños in place of the dried chili and basil leaves.

mozzarella & spinach quesadilla wedges
Prepare the basic quesadilla recipe, using a handful of baby spinach leaves in place of the basil leaves.

mozzarella & roasted red bell pepper quesadilla wedges
Prepare the basic quesadilla recipe, using 2 sliced roasted bell peppers in place of the basil leaves.

mozzarella quesadilla wedges with roasted bell pepper, basil & chili
Prepare the basic quesadilla recipe, adding 2 sliced roasted bell peppers with the chili and basil.

mozzarella & sun-dried tomato quesadilla wedges
Slice 4 drained sun-dried tomatoes. Prepare the basic quesadilla recipe, sprinkling on sun-dried tomatoes in place of the basil leaves.

variations

poppy seed grissini

see base recipe page 25

chunky breadstick twists
Prepare and roll out the basic dough, but cut it into 3/4-inch-wide strips.
Gently twist each strip and lay it on the baking sheet. Bake for about
17 minutes.

sesame seed grissini
Prepare the basic grissini recipe, using sesame seeds in place of the
poppy seeds.

parmesan grissini
Prepare the basic grissini recipe, using about 2 tablespoons freshly grated
Parmesan cheese in place of the poppy seeds.

fennel seed grissini
Prepare the basic grissini recipe, using fennel seeds in place of the
poppy seeds.

herbed garlic pita toasts

see base recipe page 26

garlic & lemon pita toasts
Prepare the basic recipe, adding 1 teaspoon grated lemon zest to the olive oil mixture.

herbed pita toasts
Prepare the basic recipe, omitting the garlic and sprinkling a mixture of chopped fresh chives, parsley, and mint over the toasts.

spicy herb pita toasts
Prepare the basic recipe, adding 1 seeded, finely chopped fresh red chili to the olive oil in place of the garlic.

garlic, herb & chili pita toasts
Prepare the basic recipe, adding 1 seeded, finely chopped red chili to the olive oil mixture.

variations

simple rice noodle crisps

see base recipe page 29

spiced rice noodle crisps
Prepare the basic recipe, adding 1 teaspoon ground coriander to the
noodle mixture.

rice noodle crisps with fennel
Prepare the basic recipe, adding 1/2 teaspoon fennel seeds to the
noodle mixture.

rice noodle crisps with cardamom
Prepare the basic recipe, adding 1/2 teaspoon crushed cardamom seeds
to the noodle mixture.

rice noodle crisps with garlic & ginger
Prepare the basic recipe, adding 1 crushed garlic clove and 1 teaspoon
grated fresh ginger to the noodle mixture.

chili cheese straws

see base recipe page 30

cheese straws
Prepare the basic recipe, omitting the chili. Lay the strips on baking sheets without twisting them.

blue cheese straws
Prepare the basic recipe, using crumbled blue cheese in place of the grated cheddar. Omit the chili and paprika.

herbed cheese straws
Prepare the basic recipe, adding 1 teaspoon chopped fresh sage leaves in place of the chili flakes.

garlic chili cheese straws
Prepare the basic recipe, adding 1 crushed garlic clove.

anchovy crackers

see base recipe page 33

sun-dried tomato & parmesan crackers
Prepare the basic recipe, using 6 chopped sun-dried tomatoes in place of
the anchovies.

anchovy & parmesan wedges
Prepare the basic recipe, chill and roll out. Instead of using a cookie cutter,
cut the dough into triangles, then bake as before.

spicy anchovy crackers
Prepare the basic recipe, adding 1/4 teaspoon dried chili flakes in place of
the black pepper.

herb & anchovy crackers
Prepare the basic recipe, adding 1 teaspoon fresh thyme leaves before
processing.

variations

beet crisps

see base recipe page 34

parsnip crisps
Use 1 to 2 parsnips in place of the beets to make sweet, golden crisps.

sweet potato crisps
Use 1 sweet potato in place of the beets to make sweet, golden-orange crisps.

pumpkin crisps
To make rich, orange crisps, use a wedge of pumpkin in place of the beets.

mixed vegetable crisps
Make multicolored crisps by using a mixture of root vegetables, such as beets, sweet potato, and potato.

variations

tortilla chips

see base recipe page 36

smoky tortilla chips
Prepare the basic recipe and dust the tortilla chips with paprika just
before serving.

tortilla chips with lime
Prepare the basic recipe and dust the tortilla chips with the finely grated
zest of 1/2 lime just before serving.

curried tortilla chips
Prepare the basic recipe and dust the tortilla chips with curry powder just
before serving.

fiery tortilla chips
Prepare the basic recipe and dust the tortilla chips with cayenne pepper just
before serving.

dips & salsas

Nothing goes better with a salty chip than a
bowlful of spicy salsa or creamy dip for dunking.
Rich and smooth, fresh and zesty, hot and spicy, or
cool and creamy — the recipes in this chapter are
perfect for laid-back munching.

creamy artichoke dip

see variations page 65

Serve this smooth, mild, and creamy dip with plain tortilla chips or breadsticks: it makes the perfect choice for those who want a reduced-fat dip.

14-oz. can artichoke hearts, drained
1 garlic clove, crushed
1 tbsp. extra virgin olive oil
1/4 tsp. ground cumin

1/4 tsp. grated lemon zest
Salt and ground black pepper
1 tbsp. chopped fresh parsley

Put the artichokes, garlic, oil, cumin, and lemon zest in a food processor. Add salt and pepper, and blend to make a smooth purée.

Check the seasoning and stir in the parsley. Scrape the dip into a bowl and serve.

Serves 4

fresh tomato & red onion salsa

see variations page 66

Fresh and tangy, this peppery tomato salsa is simple to prepare and makes a great informal summery appetizer. For a Mexican feel, serve some tortilla chips or quesadilla wedges with the dip.

3 tomatoes, seeded and finely chopped
1 red onion, quartered and finely sliced
1 green chili pepper, seeded and finely chopped
3 good pinches of ground cumin

1 tsp. red wine vinegar
1 tbsp. olive oil
Salt
2 tbsp. chopped fresh cilantro

Put the tomatoes, onion, chili pepper, cumin, vinegar, and oil in a bowl. Season with salt and toss to combine. Add the cilantro and toss again. Serve.

Serves 4

avocado salsa

see variations page 67

This classic salsa can be served as a dip with chunky dippers, such as tortilla chips, or pita wedges, for scooping.

2 avocados, peeled, pitted, and finely chopped
2 tomatoes, seeded and finely chopped
1 red chili, seeded and finely chopped
2 scallions, finely sliced

Handful of fresh cilantro, chopped
Salt
1 lime

Put the avocados, tomatoes, chili, scallions, and cilantro in a bowl. Season with salt and toss to combine.

Squeeze lime juice over the mixture to taste and toss again. Transfer the salsa to a bowl and serve within about 2 hours. Avocado discolors if it is left to stand for too long — you can minimize this by covering the surface of the salsa directly with plastic wrap, to keep the air out, and keeping the salsa chilled.

Serves 4

minty cucumber & yogurt dip

see variations page 68

This refreshing dip based on the classic Greek tzatziki makes a perfect light, informal appetizer. Serve it with pita bread or chips for scooping.

1/2 large cucumber
1 cup Greek yogurt
1 garlic clove, crushed

2 tbsp. chopped fresh mint
Salt

Peel the cucumber, cut it in half lengthways, and scrape out the seeds. Then grate the cucumber and place it in a sieve. Press out as much liquid as possible.

Place the cucumber in a bowl and mix in the yogurt, garlic, and mint. Season to taste with salt. Transfer to a serving bowl and chill until ready to serve.

Serves 4

fiery pumpkin dip

see variations page 69

This glorious orange dip offers a rich combination of sweet, spicy, fiery, and sour flavors. Be warned, once you start dipping, it's hard to stop.

1 1/2 cups (1 lb. 5 oz.) butternut squash or
    pumpkin, seeded, peeled, and cut into chunks
2 tbsp. olive oil
Salt and ground black pepper

1 garlic clove, crushed
1 tsp. grated fresh ginger
1 red chili, seeded and finely chopped
Juice of 1/2 lime

Preheat the oven to 400°F (200°C). Put the squash or pumpkin in a baking dish, drizzle with 1 tablespoon of the oil, and season with salt and pepper. Roast for about 20 minutes, tossing once or twice during cooking, until tender.

Transfer the squash or pumpkin into a food processor and add the garlic, ginger, chili, and remaining oil. Process until smooth, then briefly pulse in the lime juice and check the seasoning.

Scrape the dip into a bowl and serve hot, warm, or cold. (It will thicken on cooling, so give it a good stir before serving.)

Serves 4

zucchini & caper dip

see variations page 70

This light and tangy dip makes a healthy choice if you want a smooth, creamy dip without the calories. Serve it hot or cold with crackers or pita toasts.

3 zucchini, sliced
1/2 garlic clove, crushed
2 tsp. capers, rinsed
Good pinch of dried chili flakes

2 tbsp. olive oil
Salt
Juice of 1/4 lemon, to taste

Steam the zucchini for about 5 minutes, until tender.

Place the zucchini in a food processor and add the garlic, capers, chili, and olive oil. Process to a smooth purée. Add salt and lemon juice to taste.

Transfer the dip to a bowl and serve hot or at room temperature.

Serves 4

roasted red bell pepper & walnut dip

see variations page 71

Richly flavored with walnuts and smoky bell peppers, and served with chilled white wine, this is the perfect dip for summer barbecues.

2 large red bell peppers
1/3 cup walnuts
1/2 tsp. paprika
1/4 tsp. ground ginger
Good pinch of cayenne pepper

1 garlic clove, crushed
2 tbsp. olive oil
Salt
2 tsp. lemon juice
2 tsp. chopped fresh mint

Preheat the oven to 450°F (230°C). Place the peppers on a baking sheet and roast them for about 30 minutes, until blackened. Put the peppers in a bowl, cover with plastic wrap, and let stand for about 20 minutes, until they are cool enough to handle and the skins have loosened.

Peel and seed the peppers, then put the flesh in a food processor with the walnuts, paprika, ginger, cayenne pepper, garlic, and oil. Season with salt and process to a smooth purée.

Transfer the dip to a bowl, stir in lemon juice to taste, and adjust the seasoning. Leave to cool, then stir in the mint and serve at room temperature.

Serves 4

cannellini bean & pesto dip

see variations page 72

Whet the appetite by serving this creamy bean dip with fresh, crunchy vegetable crudités. Carrot sticks, cherry tomatoes, and strips of red bell pepper go particularly well.

14-oz. can cannellini beans, drained and rinsed	3 1/2 tbsp. basil pesto
1 garlic clove, crushed	2 tbsp. olive oil
1/4 tsp. dried chili flakes	1 tsp. lemon juice, to taste

Process the beans, garlic, chili, pesto, and oil in a food processor to make a smooth purée.

Add lemon juice to taste and process briefly, then spoon the dip into a bowl and serve.

Serves 4

beet & ginger dip

see variations page 73

Shocking pink and rich with garlic and ginger, this stunning dip is guaranteed to wake up those tastebuds and stimulate the appetite.

1 1/2 cups (9 oz.) cooked beets,
   roughly chopped
1 garlic clove, crushed
2 tsp. ground coriander

1/2 tsp. ground ginger
Salt and ground black pepper
3/4 cup Greek yogurt
1 tsp. chopped fresh mint

Put the beets, garlic, coriander, and ginger in a food processor and season with salt and pepper. Process to a smooth purée.

Add the yogurt and process briefly to combine it with the other ingredients. Check the seasoning, then scrape the dip into a bowl, sprinkle with the mint, and serve.

Serves 4

variations

creamy artichoke dip

see base recipe page 49

artichoke & chive dip
Prepare the basic recipe, adding snipped chives in place of the parsley.

artichoke dip with paprika
Prepare the basic recipe, adding a good pinch of paprika.

artichoke dip with pesto
Prepare the basic recipe, adding 1 to 2 tablespoons basil pesto in place of the lemon zest and cumin.

extra-creamy artichoke dip
Prepare the basic recipe, adding 2 tablespoons crème fraîche with the parsley.

variations

fresh tomato & red onion salsa

see base recipe page 51

fresh tomato & red onion salsa with basil
Prepare the basic recipe, replacing the cilantro with a small handful of basil.

fresh tomato, bell pepper & red onion salsa
Preheat the oven to 450°F (230°C). Place 1 red bell pepper on a baking sheet and bake for about 30 minutes, until blackened. Put the pepper in a bowl, cover with plastic wrap and leave to stand for about 10 minutes. Peel and seed the pepper, then finely chop the flesh. Prepare the basic recipe, adding the chopped red pepper with the tomatoes.

fresh tomato & mango salsa
Prepare the basic recipe, adding 1/2 peeled, pitted, and diced mango with the tomatoes.

fresh tomato & scallion salsa
Prepare the basic recipe, adding a bunch of finely sliced scallions in place of the red onion.

fresh mild tomato & red onion salsa
Prepare the basic recipe, omitting the green chili. Add a good grinding of black pepper or a pinch of paprika instead.

variations

avocado salsa

see base recipe page 52

guacamole
Using the ingredients in the basic recipe, first mash the avocados to make a smooth paste, then fold in the other ingredients and season with salt and lime juice to taste.

avocado & kiwi salsa
Prepare the basic recipe, adding 1 peeled, finely chopped kiwi fruit with the cilantro.

avocado & mango salsa
Prepare the basic recipe, adding 1/2 peeled, pitted, and finely chopped mango with the avocado.

mild avocado salsa
Prepare the basic recipe, omitting the chili. Add a good grinding of black pepper and a pinch of ground cumin instead.

avocado & red bell pepper salsa
Prepare the basic recipe, adding 1/2 seeded and finely chopped red bell pepper with the avocado.

variations

minty cucumber & yogurt dip

see base recipe page 55

garlicky cucumber & yogurt dip
Prepare the basic recipe, adding an extra clove of crushed garlic.

spicy cucumber & yogurt dip
Prepare the basic recipe, adding 1 seeded and finely chopped green chili.

cucumber, scallion & yogurt dip
Prepare the basic recipe, adding 3 finely sliced scallions.

herb, cucumber & mint dip
Prepare the basic recipe, adding 1 tablespoon snipped fresh chives and 1 tablespoon chopped fresh cilantro with the mint.

fiery pumpkin dip

see base recipe page 56

chunky pumpkin dip
Instead of using a food processor, coarsely mash the squash or pumpkin by hand and stir in the other ingredients to produce a chunkier dip.

spiced pumpkin dip
Prepare the basic recipe, omitting the chili. Add 1 teaspoon ground cumin and 1 teaspoon ground coriander with the garlic and ginger.

curried pumpkin dip
Prepare the basic recipe, adding 1 teaspoon medium curry paste to the cooked pumpkin and the juice of 1/2 to 1 lemon instead of the lime juice.

spicy pumpkin dip with harissa
Prepare the basic recipe, omitting the chili and adding 1 teaspoon harissa (hot chili paste) and 1 teaspoon ground cumin instead.

variations

zucchini & caper dip

see base recipe page 59

lemon zucchini & caper dip
Prepare the basic recipe, adding 1/2 teaspoon grated lemon zest with
the lemon juice.

creamy zucchini & caper dip
Prepare the basic recipe, omitting the chili flakes and adding 3 tablespoons
crème fraîche with the lemon juice.

zucchini, caper & dill dip
Prepare the basic recipe, adding 1 tablespoon chopped fresh dill and
2 tablespoons crème fraîche with the lemon juice.

minted zucchini & caper dip
Prepare the basic recipe, adding 1 teaspoon chopped fresh mint to the
food processor. Sprinkle with extra chopped fresh mint before serving.

zucchini, caper & parsley dip
Prepare the basic recipe, adding 2 tablespoons chopped fresh parsley
to the food processor. Sprinkle with more parsley when serving.

roasted red bell pepper & walnut dip

see base recipe page 60

creamy roasted bell pepper dip
Prepare the basic recipe, then stir in 3 tablespoons crème fraîche when the dip has cooled.

roasted red bell pepper & cashew dip
Prepare the basic recipe using cashews in place of the walnuts.

roasted red bell pepper & walnut dip with basil
Prepare the basic recipe, adding a small handful of fresh basil leaves to the food processor, and omitting the mint.

roasted red bell pepper with pine nuts & basil
Prepare the basic recipe, using pine nuts in place of the walnuts and adding a small handful of fresh basil leaves. Omit the mint.

variations

cannellini bean & pesto dip

see base recipe page 63

kidney bean & red pesto dip
Prepare the basic recipe using kidney beans in place of the cannellini beans, and red pesto in place of green pesto.

cannellini bean & zucchini dip
Slice 1 zucchini and steam the slices over boiling water for about 5 minutes, until tender. Prepare the basic recipe, adding the steamed zucchini with the beans, and process to make a smooth dip.

cannellini bean & roasted bell pepper dip
Prepare the basic recipe, adding 2 drained bottled roasted bell peppers with the beans.

extra-creamy bean dip
Prepare the basic dip and stir in 2 tablespoons crème fraîche with the lemon juice.

variations

beet & ginger dip

see base recipe page 64

beet, orange & ginger dip
Prepare the basic recipe, adding the grated zest of 1/2 orange with
the yogurt.

spicy beet & ginger dip
Prepare the basic recipe, adding 1 teaspoon harissa (hot chili paste) or
1 teaspoon paprika and a good pinch of cayenne pepper.

beet & ginger dip with chives
Prepare the basic recipe, and sprinkle with snipped chives in place
of the mint.

beet & ginger dip with cilantro
Prepare the basic dip and sprinkle with chopped fresh cilantro
in place of the mint.

mini mouthfuls

Good things come in small packages, and these tiny snacks pack a hearty punch. From nuts to cheese, olives to mushrooms, no-one will be able to resist taking just one more of these tiny morsels — each one designed to make the mouth water.

marinated olives

see variations page 91

A bowl of fragrant, marinated olives is all you need to whet the appetite. Whether simple or sophisticated, they are utterly irresistible every time.

2 garlic cloves, sliced
Good pinch of dried chili flakes
1 tsp. chopped fresh rosemary
1 tbsp. chopped fresh flat-leaf parsley

1 tbsp. red wine vinegar
2 tbsp. olive oil
2 1/4 cups (9 oz.) black or green olives

Whisk together the garlic, dried chili, rosemary, parsley, vinegar, and olive oil in a bowl large enough to hold the olives.

Add the olives to the marinade and toss to coat them thoroughly. Cover and chill for at least 4 hours before serving. The olives will keep well for 3 to 4 days in the refrigerator.

Serves 4

quail's eggs with
black olive tapenade

see variations page 92

Tiny quail's eggs are delicious dipped into the salty, pungent black olive and anchovy paste known as tapenade. They are perfect with pre-dinner drinks.

12 quail's eggs
1 3/4 cups (7 oz.) pitted black olives
2 garlic cloves, crushed
3 anchovies

2 tsp. capers, rinsed and drained
1–2 tbsp. olive oil
Black pepper
Squeeze of lemon juice

Bring a pan of water to a boil. Gently add the quail's eggs and boil for 4 minutes. Drain the eggs, return them to the pan, and cover with cold water. Leave to cool.

For the tapenade, put the olives, garlic, anchovies, capers, and olive oil in a food processor. Season with black pepper and process to a smooth purée. Add lemon juice to taste. Scrape the tapenade into a small dish and place on a serving platter.

Half-shell the eggs, leaving a neat base of shell to hold. Arrange them around the dish of tapenade and serve.

Serves 4

smoky spiced almonds

see variations page 93

Serve these crisp, smoky nuts the Spanish way, with a glass of chilled sherry or a tall cool glass of beer.

1 tsp. olive oil
1 1/3 cups (7 oz.) blanched almonds

Coarse sea salt
1/4 tsp. paprika

Heat the olive oil in a large nonstick pan, then add the almonds and toss over the heat for about 5 minutes, until golden.

Use a slotted spoon to transfer the nuts to a bowl, leaving as much oil in the pan as possible. Sprinkle generously with coarse sea salt and paprika, and toss the nuts to coat them in the seasoning. Cool, then transfer to a serving dish.

Serves 4–8

garlic mushrooms

see variations page 94

Serve these juicy, flavorsome mouthfuls of garlic mushrooms with toothpicks so your guests can pick them up and pop them into their mouths without getting their fingers sticky.

1 1/2 tbsp. olive oil
2 garlic cloves, crushed
2 2/3 cups (7 oz.) button mushrooms
2 tbsp. white wine

1 tsp. tomato paste
1/2 tsp. fresh thyme leaves, plus extra for
    garnishing
Salt and ground black pepper

Pour the olive oil into a frying pan. Gently fry the garlic in the oil for about 1 minute, then add the mushrooms and toss to coat in the oil.

Stir the wine and tomato paste together and pour over the mushrooms, then add the thyme and season with salt and pepper. Cook gently for 15 to 20 minutes, stirring occasionally, until most of the juices have evaporated and the mushrooms are juicy and glossy but not wet.

Transfer to a serving dish. Serve hot, warm, or at room temperature, sprinkled with a few fresh thyme leaves.

Serves 4

spicy shrimp skewers

see variations page 95

With a fresh, zesty flavor, these simple skewers make a great informal appetizer to serve with drinks. For a more formal first course, serve the skewers on a lightly dressed salad.

1 tsp. grated fresh root ginger
1 garlic clove, crushed
Grated zest of 1/2 lime and juice of 1 lime
Salt and ground black pepper

16–20 raw tiger shrimp, peeled and deveined
Chopped fresh mint, for sprinkling
Sweet chili sauce, for dipping

Soak twelve short bamboo skewers in water for 10 to 20 minutes. Mix the ginger, garlic, and lime zest and juice in a large bowl and season with salt and pepper. Add the shrimp, toss to coat them in the seasonings, and cover. Chill for about 5 to 10 minutes.

Preheat the broiler, or heat a ridged griddle pan. Thread a shrimp lengthwise onto the end of each skewer. Arrange the shrimp on the broiler pan or griddle and cook for about 1 minute on each side, until pink and cooked through.

Transfer the cooked shrimp to a platter and sprinkle with mint. Serve immediately, with chili sauce for dipping.

Serves 4

prosciutto-wrapped asparagus with lemon mayo

see variations page 96

These sophisticated bites make an irresistible nibble with aperitifs or as a more formal appetizer. You can prepare everything ahead, then simply pop them in the oven when your guests arrive.

1/2 cup mayonnaise
Grated zest of 1 lemon
1 tbsp. fresh lemon juice
1/2 tbsp. snipped fresh chives

8 asparagus tips
8 wafer-thin slices prosciutto, cut into strips
Olive oil, for drizzling
Ground black pepper

Preheat the oven to 375°F (190°C). Combine the mayonnaise, lemon zest, juice, and chives in a serving dish. Cover and place in the refrigerator.

Wrap each asparagus tip in a strip of prosciutto, arrange on a baking sheet, and drizzle with the oil. Sprinkle with a little black pepper and roast for 6 to 7 minutes, until tender.

Transfer the prosciutto-wrapped asparagus to a platter and serve with the lemon mayo.

Serves 4

bocconcini with mint & chili

see variations page 97

You can buy bocconcini, bite-size balls of mozzarella, in most good cheese shops, larger supermarkets, and delis. Alternatively, buy a block of regular mozzarella and cut it into bite-size pieces.

9 oz. bocconcini mozzarella
1/4 tsp. dried chili flakes

1 tsp. chopped fresh mint
1 1/2 tbsp. extra virgin olive oil

Drain the bocconcini and place in a bowl. Sprinkle with the chili and mint and drizzle with the oil. Toss to coat each ball well.

Cover and leave to marinate in the refrigerator for at least 1 hour. Allow the cheese to return to room temperature before serving.

Serves 4

tomato & mozzarella skewers

see variations page 98

These pretty red-and-white skewers take no time to put together. The salsa is also quick to whip up, and you can make it in advance to save time when guests arrive.

2 handfuls fresh basil leaves
2 tsp. capers, drained and rinsed
1/2 tsp. Dijon mustard
1 1/2 tsp. balsamic vinegar

4 tbsp. olive oil
Ground black pepper
1/4 lb. mozzarella, drained
20 cherry tomatoes

To make the salsa, put the basil leaves, capers, mustard, vinegar, and olive oil in a small blender, season with black pepper, and process until smooth. Transfer the mixture to a serving bowl, cover, and — if preparing ahead — chill until ready to serve.

Cut the mozarella into 20 bite-size cubes. Thread onto cocktail skewers with a cherry tomato. Arrange the skewers on a serving platter with the salsa for dipping.

Makes 20

feta & watermelon spikes

see variations page 99

These little mouthfuls are refreshing, salty, and piquant. They are perfect taste-teasers before a meal on a hot summer afternoon or evening.

Small wedge of watermelon (about 1 lb.),
    chilled
7 oz. feta cheese

A little lime juice
Ground black pepper

Peel the watermelon and remove the black seeds, then cut the flesh into 24 bite-size chunks. Cut the cheese into 24 bite-size cubes.

Skewer a cube of cheese and a cube of watermelon onto each toothpick. Squeeze a little lime juice over the skewers, sprinkle with black pepper, and serve.

Makes 24

marinated olives

see base recipe page 75

red-hot marinated olives
Prepare the basic recipe, omitting the crushed dried chili and adding 1 fresh sliced red chili instead. Remove and discard the chili seeds before slicing for a slightly milder result.

fragrant marinated olives
Prepare the basic recipe, adding 1/2 teaspoon crushed, toasted coriander seeds.

marinated olives with oregano
Prepare the basic recipe, omitting the rosemary and adding 1 teaspoon crushed oregano instead.

cumin-spiced olives
Prepare the basic recipe, replacing the rosemary with 1/2 teaspoon ground cumin.

marinated olives with fresh mint
Prepare the basic recipe, omitting the rosemary and adding 1 teaspoon chopped fresh mint instead.

quail's eggs with black olive tapenade

see base recipe page 77

quail's eggs with herb tapenade

Prepare the basic recipe, adding 1/2 teaspoon chopped fresh marjoram to the tapenade before blending.

crostini with tapenade & quail's eggs

Prepare the basic recipe. Cut 12 thin slices off a small baguette and toast them on both sides until golden. Spread each piece of toast with a thin layer of tapenade, top with a shelled, halved quail's egg, and serve sprinkled with chopped parsley.

quail's eggs with creamy tapenade

Prepare the basic recipe, omitting the lemon juice. Gradually stir the tapenade into 1/2 cup cream cheese. Then add lemon juice to taste. Add more cream cheese for a lighter-flavored dip.

quail's eggs with lemon & tarragon tapenade

Prepare the basic recipe, adding 2 tablespoons chopped fresh tarragon and the grated zest of 1 lemon with the lemon juice.

variations

smoky spiced almonds

see base recipe page 78

almonds & raisins
Prepare the basic recipe. When the nuts are cool, toss in a handful of plump, juicy raisins.

mixed spiced nuts
Prepare the basic recipe using a mixture of plain unsalted nuts, such as almonds, cashews, and pecans.

toasted nuts & raisins
Prepare the basic recipe using a mixture of plain unsalted nuts, such as almonds, cashews, and blanched hazelnuts, and omitting the paprika. When the nuts are cool, toss in a handful of plump, juicy raisins.

curried cashews
Prepare the basic recipe using cashews instead of almonds, and curry powder in place of the paprika.

toasted nuts & seeds
Prepare the basic recipe using a mixture of nuts and seeds such as almonds, cashews, pecans, pumpkin seeds, and sunflower seeds.

variations

garlic mushrooms

see base recipe page 81

spicy garlic mushrooms
Prepare the basic recipe, adding a good pinch of dried chili flakes with the mushrooms.

garlic mushrooms and chives
Prepare the basic recipe, omitting the thyme. Serve the mushrooms sprinkled with 1 tablespoon snipped fresh chives.

garlic mushrooms with sherry & oregano
Prepare the basic recipe using sherry in place of the white wine, and 1/2 teaspoon chopped fresh oregano in place of the thyme.

creamy garlic mushrooms
Prepare the basic recipe, then stir 1 tablespoon heavy cream into the mushrooms before serving. Best served hot or warm.

garlic mushrooms with bay leaf
Prepare the basic recipe, adding a bay leaf to the pan with the wine and thyme. Leave the bay leaf in with the mushrooms while they are cooling, then remove it before serving.

spicy shrimp skewers

see base recipe page 82

chili shrimp
Prepare the basic recipe, adding 1 finely chopped seeded red chili pepper
to the marinade.

sweet chili shrimp
Prepare the basic recipe, using 2 tablespoons sweet chili sauce in place of
the lime zest and juice.

coconut shrimp
Prepare the basic recipe. Before cooking, roll the skewered shrimp in 2
tablespoons grated coconut, then broil as before.

cilantro shrimp
Prepare the basic recipe, sprinkling the cooked shrimp with 1 tablespoon
chopped fresh cilantro instead of the mint before serving.

variations

prosciutto-wrapped asparagus with lemon mayo

see base recipe page 85

roasted asparagus with lemon mayonnaise
Prepare the basic recipe, omitting the prosciutto.

prosciutto-wrapped asparagus with garlic mayonnaise
Prepare the basic recipe, adding 1 small crushed garlic clove to the
mayonnaise and using chopped fresh parsley instead of chives.

prosciutto-wrapped asparagus with caper mayonnaise
Prepare the basic recipe, adding 1 teaspoon chopped capers to
the mayonnaise.

prosciutto-wrapped asparagus with coriander mayonnaise
Prepare the basic recipe, using grated lime zest and juice in place of the
lemon zest and juice, and 1 tablespoon chopped fresh coriander in place of
the chives.

prosciutto-wrapped asparagus with spicy mayonnaise
Prepare the basic recipe, using 1/2 to 1 teaspoon harissa (hot chili paste) in
place of the chives.

bocconcini with mint & chili

see base recipe page 86

bocconcini with fennel seeds
Prepare the basic recipe, adding 1/2 teaspoon lightly crushed fennel seeds.

bocconcini with garlic
Prepare the basic recipe, adding 1/2 crushed garlic clove.

bocconcini with basil & chili
Prepare the basic recipe, adding a small handful of torn fresh basil leaves
in place of the mint.

bocconcini with sage & chili
Prepare the basic recipe, replacing the mint with 1/2 teaspoon chopped
fresh sage.

variations

tomato & mozzarella skewers

see base recipe page 89

tomato, mozzarella & olive skewers
Prepare the basic recipe, adding a pitted black olive to each toothpick.

tomato & mozzarella skewers with arugula
Prepare the basic recipe, threading 1 or 2 arugula leaves on each toothpick.

tomato, mozzarella & avocado skewers
Peel and stone half an avocado, then slice the flesh into 20 bite-size pieces.
Prepare the basic recipe, adding a cube of avocado to each toothpick.

tomato & mozzarella skewers with red onion
Cut half a red onion into quarters, then separate the quarters into layers.
Prepare the basic recipe, threading a slice of onion onto each toothpick.

variations

feta & watermelon spikes

see base recipe page 90

feta, black olive & watermelon spikes
Prepare the basic recipe, adding a pitted black olive to each toothpick.

feta & cantaloupe spikes
Prepare the basic recipe, using cantaloupe in place of the watermelon.

brie & grape spikes
Following the basic method, thread each toothpick with a cube of brie and a
large red seedless grape in place of the watermelon and feta.
Omit the lime juice.

blue cheese & pear spikes
Peel, core, and slice 2 ripe pears into 24 thin wedges. Following the basic
method, thread cocktail sticks with a cube of blue cheese and a slice of pear.
Omit the lime juice.

blue cheese & fig spikes
Prepare 4 figs, slicing each into 6 wedges. Following the basic method,
thread cocktail sticks with a cube of blue cheese and a wedge of fig.
Omit the lime juice.

big bites

One look at these big tempting treats and your guests will be begging for the recipes. Serve them when your guests are starving hungry, to keep them going until the main meal.

spicy chicken wings

see variations page 117

Golden fried chicken wings are everyone's favorite and great for a party snack to offer before the main food event. For a more formal meal, serve these with a dressed salad and a dipping sauce.

2 tbsp. all-purpose flour
2 tsp. cayenne pepper
Salt

12 chicken wings
Sunflower oil, for deep-frying

Put the flour, cayenne pepper, and a good pinch of salt in an insulated or plastic bag and shake to mix. Add the chicken wings and shake to coat them in the seasoned flour.

Pour oil into a deep pan until it is two-thirds full. Heat to 375°F (190°C) or until a cube of bread turns brown in about 1 minute. Add the chicken wings, 3 to 4 at a time, and fry for about 10 minutes until golden brown and cooked through.

Drain the wings on paper towels and keep the cooked batches hot while you cook the remaining chicken wings the same way. Serve hot.

Makes 12

cheese garlic bread

see variations page 118

Richly flavored garlic bread makes a feel-good starter when you need a little treat. Serve these little breads before an Italian main course or offer them from a platter with drinks at a party.

for the dough
1 3/4 cups white bread flour
1 tsp. dry yeast
1/2 tsp. salt
1 tbsp. olive oil
1/2 cup warm water

for the topping
2 tbsp. olive oil
2 garlic cloves, crushed
5 oz. mozzarella, thinly sliced
Ground black pepper
Chopped fresh parsley, for sprinkling

Combine the flour, yeast, and salt in a large bowl, and make a well in the middle. Add the oil and water and mix to a soft dough. Turn out the dough on to a lightly floured surface and knead for 5 to 10 minutes until smooth and elastic. Place in a clean oiled bowl, cover with oiled plastic wrap, and let rise in a warm place for about 1 hour, or until doubled in bulk.

Preheat the oven to 425°F (220°C) and lightly grease a baking sheet. Divide the dough into 8 pieces and roll into rounds or ovals, arranging them slightly apart on the baking sheet.

Mix the oil and garlic, then drizzle it over the bread. Top with the cheese, season with pepper, and bake for about 12 minutes, until golden and bubbling. Serve immediately, sprinkled with fresh parsley.

Makes 8

mini pizzas with sweet bell peppers & mozzarella

see variations page 119

These delicious mini-pizzas, topped with a rich sweet pepper sauce, are a great twist on the classic tomato pizza.

1 quantity bread dough (as for cheese garlic
    bread, page 103)
2 tbsp. olive oil
2 garlic cloves, crushed
2 red bell peppers, seeded and chopped

1 handful basil leaves
1 tsp. balsamic vinegar
5 1/2 oz. mozzarella, sliced
Salt and ground black pepper
2 handfuls arugula

Prepare the bread dough and leave to rise. Meanwhile, heat the oil in a frying pan. Add the garlic and peppers and fry gently for about 20 minutes, stirring frequently, until tender. Transfer the garlic and pepper mixture to a food processor, add the basil and balsamic vinegar, and process until smooth. Season to taste and set aside.

Preheat the oven to 425°F (220°C) and grease a baking sheet. Knead the risen dough briefly, cut it into 8 pieces, and roll the pieces into rounds, laying them slightly apart on the baking sheet. Spread about 1 tablespoon of the pepper mixture over each dough round, then top with 1 to 2 slices of mozzarella and season with pepper. Bake for about 10 minutes, until golden and bubbling. Top the mini pizzas with arugula and serve immediately.

Makes 8

deep-fried risotto balls with melting mozzarella

see variations page 120

These rich, creamy risotto balls filled with basil and melting mozzarella are an indulgent feast of an appetizer. Serve them with a fresh, tangy tomato or fruit salsa.

2 tbsp. olive oil
1 small onion, finely chopped
1 garlic clove, crushed
2/3 cup risotto rice
1/3 cup white wine
1 2/3 cups boiling vegetable or chicken stock

1/3 cup grated Parmesan cheese
2 tbsp. chopped fresh flat-leaf parsley
3 oz. mozzarella, cut into 12 small cubes
12 large basil leaves
Sunflower oil, for deep-frying
Salt and freshly ground black pepper

Heat the oil in a large pan, then gently fry the onion and garlic for about 4 minutes, until soft but not brown. Add the rice, stir for 2 minutes, pour in the wine and simmer, stirring, until absorbed. Add the stock and stir frequently for about 20 minutes, until the stock is absorbed and the risotto is creamy. Stir in the Parmesan, parsley and seasoning. Let cool.

Divide the cooled rice into 12 portions. Wrap each cube of mozzarella in a basil leaf. Press a portion of rice around each cube. Place on a board and let stand for at least 30 minutes. Pour oil into a deep pan until it is two-thirds full. Heat the oil to 375°F (190°C), or until a cube of bread turns brown in about 1 minute. Deep-fry the risotto balls in batches, for about 3 minutes, until crisp and golden. Drain on paper towels and serve hot.

Serves 4

sun-dried tomato frittata

see variations page 121

This thick, Italian-style omelet is delicious served in wedges as a chunky snack, with pre-dinner drinks, or with a salad as a formal appetizer.

2 tbsp. olive oil
1 Spanish onion, thinly sliced
Salt
1 tsp. fresh thyme leaves

6 sun-dried tomatoes in oil, drained and sliced
1/3 cup freshly grated Parmesan cheese
6 eggs, beaten
Ground black pepper

Heat the oil in a large frying pan. Add the onion, sprinkle with a little salt and the thyme, and fry gently for about 15 minutes. Stir in the tomatoes and season to taste.

Stir the Parmesan into the eggs and season with black pepper. Pour the egg mixture over the onions and cook gently for 5 to 10 minutes, until the frittata is firm but still moist on top. Lift the edges of the frittata occasionally to allow uncooked egg to run underneath.

Preheat the broiler. Brown the top of the frittata under the broiler for 3 to 5 minutes. Serve hot, warm, or at room temperature, cut into wedges.

Serves 6

caramelized onion & anchovy squares

see variations page 122

Based on the classic French *pissaladière*, these melting squares of puff pastry make a chunky, satisfying appetizer to hand around with drinks.

2 tbsp. olive oil	2 tsp. brown sugar
1 large Spanish onion, halved and thinly sliced	13-oz. package ready-rolled puff pastry
Salt and black pepper	2-oz. can anchovies, drained and halved
1 tsp. fresh thyme leaves, plus extra for garnish	lengthwise

Heat the oil in a pan. Add the onion, season with salt and pepper, and sprinkle with thyme. Cook gently, stirring occasionally, for about 20 minutes, until the onion is soft and tender. Sprinkle in the brown sugar and cook for a further 10 minutes, stirring more frequently, until the onion is golden and sticky. Check the seasoning.

Meanwhile, preheat the oven to 375°F (190°C). Unroll the pastry onto a large baking sheet. Spread the onion on the pastry, then arrange the anchovies in a lattice pattern over the top.

Bake for about 25 minutes, until the pastry is crisp and golden. Cut the pastry into 12 squares or rectangles and serve hot, warm, or at room temperature, sprinkled with more fresh thyme.

Makes 12

potato wedges with crème fraîche & pesto dip

see variations page 123

These are firm favorites with drinks or for a laid-back dinner. Depending on the pesto, you may need to add a teaspoonful more to the dip: taste it first and add a little more if needed.

2 large potatoes (about 1 lb. 5 oz.)
2 tbsp. olive oil
Salt and ground black pepper

1/2 cup crème fraîche
About 1 tbsp. basil pesto

Preheat the oven to 375°F (190°C). Cut the potatoes into chunky wedges and place in a roasting pan, in a single layer. Drizzle with the oil, season with salt and pepper, and toss to combine.

Bake the potatoes for 30 to 35 minutes, until golden and tender, shaking and turning them once or twice.

Meanwhile, mix the crème fraîche and pesto in a serving bowl, and season with black pepper. Serve the freshly cooked potato wedges with the dip.

Serves 4

baked camembert

see variations page 124

This recipe is a stunningly simple twist on the classic Swiss fondue. It's perfect in winter, when everyone's cold and hungry.

1 camembert in a wooden box   **1 medium baguette**

Preheat the oven to 375°F (190°C). Discard the waxed paper from around the cheese and return it to its box. Place on a baking sheet and bake for about 20 minutes.

Cut the baguette into bite-size chunks. Transfer the cheese, in its box, to a serving plate. Break a hole in the crust of the cheese and invite everyone to spike chunks of bread on forks and dunk them into the melted cheese.

Serves 4

grilled polenta with blue cheese & arugula

see variations page 125

This hearty appetizer is particularly good in winter when you need something filling to warm you up. Quick-cook polenta speeds up the preparation, but you can use regular polenta instead, following the instructions on the packet.

2 cups water
1/4 tsp. salt
3/4 cup quick-cook polenta
1 tbsp. olive oil, plus extra for brushing
2 tsp. balsamic vinegar

1/2 tsp. whole-grain mustard
2 oz. gorgonzola or other blue cheese, thinly
  sliced
2 handfuls arugula
Ground black pepper

Bring the water and salt to a boil. Slowly add the polenta, stirring, and cook for about 3 minutes, until thick. Pour the polenta onto a board or tray and spread out to about 3/4 inch thick, then leave to cool. Whisk together the oil, vinegar, and mustard, and set aside.

Preheat a griddle. Using a 2 3/4-inch cookie cutter, cut the polenta into eight rounds and brush each side with oil. Arrange the polenta rounds on the griddle and cook for 4 to 5 minutes, until charred with dark lines. Flip over, top with cheese, and cook for a further 3 to 4 minutes. Transfer the polenta to serving plates, top with arugula, and drizzle with the dressing. Grind a little black pepper over the polenta and serve.

Serves 4

variations

spicy chicken wings

see base recipe page 101

hot ginger chicken wings
Prepare the basic recipe, adding 1 teaspoon ground ginger to the flour.

smoky chicken wings
Prepare the basic recipe, adding 2 teaspoons paprika to the flour in place
of the cayenne pepper.

warmly spiced chicken wings
Prepare the basic recipe, adding 2 teaspoons ground cumin, 2 teaspoons
ground coriander, 1 teaspoon paprika, and 1/2 teaspoon dried chili flakes
to the flour in place of the cayenne pepper.

curried chicken wings
Prepare the basic recipe, adding 2 teaspoons curry powder to the flour.

variations

cheese garlic bread

see base recipe page 103

plain garlic bread
Prepare the basic dough rounds and slash the top of each one several times with a sharp knife. Bake for about 12 minutes. Meanwhile, combine 1/4 cup (1/2 stick) soft butter with 2 crushed garlic cloves and season with black pepper. When the breads are cooked, spread with the garlic butter and sprinkle with parsley.

herb & cheese garlic bread
Prepare the basic recipe, sprinkling the bread with fresh thyme leaves or snipped chives instead of parsley.

cheese garlic bread with pesto
Prepare the basic recipe, spreading about 1/2 teaspoon pesto on each dough round before drizzling with the garlic oil.

cheese garlic bread with chili
Prepare the basic recipe, sprinkling a good pinch of dried chili flakes over each bread before baking.

mini pizzas with sweet bell peppers & mozzarella

see base recipe page 104

mini pizzas with sweet bell peppers, mozzarella & spicy sausage
Prepare the basic recipe, scattering a few slices of chorizo or other spicy sausage on top before baking. Serve with or without arugula.

mini pizzas with sweet bell peppers, mozzarella & chargrilled zucchini
Slice a zucchini and brush with olive oil, then cook on a griddle for about 4 minutes on each side, until charred and tender. Prepare the basic pizza recipe, scattering over the zucchini slices before baking. Serve without arugula.

mini pizzas with sweet bell peppers, mozzarella & olives
Prepare the basic recipe, scattering a few olives on top of each pizza before baking. Serve with or without arugula.

mini pizzas with sweet bell peppers, mozzarella, capers & pine nuts
Prepare the basic recipe, sprinkling 2 teaspoons drained and rinsed capers and 1 tablespoon pine nuts over the pizzas before baking. Serve with or without arugula.

variations

deep-fried risotto balls with melting mozzarella

see base recipe page 107

deep-fried risotto balls with chives & mozzarella
Prepare the basic recipe, adding 2 tablespoons snipped fresh chives in place of the parsley. Omit the basil leaves from the filling.

deep-fried risotto balls with sage & mozzarella
Prepare the basic recipe, adding 2 teaspoons chopped fresh sage in place of the parsley. Omit the basil leaves from the filling.

deep-fried risotto balls with melting blue cheese
Prepare the basic recipe, using cubes of blue cheese in place of the mozzarella. Omit the basil leaves from the filling.

deep-fried herbed risotto balls with melting mozzarella
Prepare the basic recipe, stirring 2 tablespoons snipped fresh chives and 2 teaspoons chopped fresh mint into the risotto with the parsley.

variations

sun-dried tomato frittata

see base recipe page 108

leek & sun-dried tomato frittata
Prepare the basic recipe, using 2 sliced leeks in place of the Spanish onion.

roasted bell pepper frittata
Prepare the basic recipe, adding 3 sliced roasted bell peppers along with
the tomatoes.

sun-dried tomato & sage frittata
Prepare the basic recipe, omitting the thyme and adding 1/2 teaspoon
chopped fresh sage to the beaten eggs.

spicy sun-dried tomato frittata
Prepare the basic recipe, cooking 1 to 2 chopped fresh red chilies with
the onions.

variations

caramelized onion & anchovy squares

see base recipe page 111

caramelized onion & anchovy squares with golden raisins
Prepare the basic recipe and sprinkle a handful of golden raisins over the tart about 10 minutes before the end of the cooking time.

caramelized onion & anchovy squares with parmesan shavings
Prepare the basic recipe, scattering the squares with Parmesan shavings just before serving.

caramelized onion & anchovy squares with olives
Prepare the basic recipe, scattering a handful of pitted black olives over the tart before baking.

caramelized onion & anchovy squares with oregano
Prepare the basic recipe, using oregano in place of thyme.

caramelized onion squares with prosciutto
Snip 4 slices of prosciutto into pieces. Prepare the basic recipe, omitting the anchovies, and scatter the prosciutto over the top about 10 minutes before the end of the cooking time.

variations

potato wedges with crème fraîche & pesto dip

see base recipe page 112

spicy potato wedges with crème fraîche & pesto dip
Prepare the basic recipe, adding 1 teaspoon crushed dried chili and
1 teaspoon ground cumin to the oil before drizzling it over the potatoes.

potato wedges with tarragon mayonnaise
Prepare the basic recipe, using mayonnaise in place of the crème fraîche and
adding 2 tablespoons chopped fresh tarragon and 1 teaspoon grated lemon
zest instead of the pesto.

potato wedges with with crème fraîche & red pesto dip
Prepare the basic recipe, using red pesto in place of green pesto.

potato wedges with lemon mayonnaise
Prepare the basic recipe, using mayonnaise in place of the crème fraîche and
adding 1 teaspoon grated lemon zest and 2 teaspoons lemon juice instead
of the pesto.

potato wedges with spicy lemon mayonnaise
Prepare the basic recipe, using mayonnaise in place of the crème fraîche and
adding 2 teaspoons grated lemon zest and several good splashes of Tabasco
instead of the pesto.

variations

baked camembert

see base recipe page 115

baked camembert with new potatoes
Prepare the basic recipe, serving the cheese with boiled baby new potatoes in place of the baguette.

baked camembert with breadsticks
Prepare the basic recipe, serving the cheese with chunky breadsticks instead of a baguette.

baked camembert with cherry tomatoes
Prepare the basic recipe, serving the cheese with cherry tomatoes in place of the bread.

baked camembert with garlic toasts
Prepare the basic recipe. Instead of serving the baguette in chunks, slice it and toast it on both sides until golden. Rub each slice with a cut clove of garlic and serve.

baked vacherin
Prepare the basic recipe, using a vacherin in place of the camembert.

grilled polenta with blue cheese & arugula

see base recipe page 116

grilled polenta with blue cheese & baby spinach leaves
Prepare the basic recipe, using baby spinach leaves in place of the arugula.

grilled polenta with blue cheese & cherry tomatoes
Prepare the basic recipe, topping each slice with a few halved cherry tomatoes.

grilled polenta with blue cheese & pear
Prepare the basic recipe, topping each slice with a wedge or two of peeled, cored pear.

grilled polenta with blue cheese & fig
Prepare the basic recipe, topping each slice with a wedge or two of fresh fig.

tapas tasters

Designed as little morsels to serve with drinks, these

Spanish-style appetizers are perfect for whetting

the appetite and are guaranteed to get a party

going with a swing. Prepare a selection and let

guests pick and choose.

mini meatballs

see variations page 142

These richly flavored meatballs make a tempting informal appetizer. If you're handing them out with drinks, serve them with toothpicks for skewering. If you're serving them at the table, serve chunks of bread for mopping up the luscious sauce.

6 oz. lean ground beef
1/4 onion, grated
1/2 garlic clove, crushed
1 tsp. chopped fresh oregano
1 tbsp. grated Parmesan cheese

1 tbsp. olive oil
8 oz. drained canned or fresh tomatoes, peeled
and chopped
Salt and ground black pepper

Combine the beef, onion, garlic, half the oregano, and the Parmesan cheese in a bowl. Season well and mix thoroughly. Roll the mixture into about 20 bite-size balls.

Heat the oil in a large, nonstick frying pan. Add the meatballs and cook, stirring them gently to brown them all over. Work in batches if necessary, removing browned meatballs as they are ready. When all the meatballs are browned, return them to the pan.

Add the tomatoes and remaining oregano, season with salt and pepper, and simmer gently for about 20 minutes, until the meatballs are cooked and tender. Serve hot or warm.

Serves 4

broiled mussels

see variations page 143

The Spanish love shellfish and this simple yet sophisticated appetizer really makes the most of fresh mussels.

1 lb. 2 oz. mussels, cleaned
4 tbsp. dry bread crumbs
3 tbsp. freshly grated Parmesan cheese
2 garlic cloves, crushed

2 tbsp. chopped fresh parsley
2 1/2 tbsp. olive oil
Ground black pepper

Check the mussels, discarding any that are open or ones that do not close when sharply tapped. Put the closed mussels in a large pan, add 3 tablespoons water, cover tightly, and cook over high heat for about 5 minutes, shaking the pan frequently, until the mussels have opened.

Discard any unopened shells. Snap off and discard the top shell of each mussel and arrange the shells with mussels in a flameproof dish.

Preheat the broiler. Combine the breadcrumbs, Parmesan cheese, garlic, parsley, and oil, and season with black pepper. Spoon the crumb mixture onto the mussels, then broil them for about 2 minutes until golden and bubbling. Serve immediately.

Serves 4

garlic & chili shrimp

see variations page 144

Serve these delectable shrimp with chunks of crusty bread for soaking up the garlic and chili-infused oil.

3 tbsp. olive oil
1 garlic clove, crushed
1/4 tsp. dried chili flakes

20 raw tiger shrimp (with shells on)
Chunks of crusty bread, to serve

Heat the oil in a large frying pan and fry the garlic and chili for about 1 minute, until aromatic. Add the shrimp and cook for a further 3 to 4 minutes, turning them occasionally, until they are pink and cooked through.

Transfer the shrimp to plates. Drizzle the oil from the pan over them and serve immediately, with chunks of bread to mop up the oil.

Serves 4

green pea tortilla

see variations page 145

This tortilla is great to serve in bite-size pieces with drinks or with a simple salad as a more formal appetizer.

2 tbsp. olive oil
2 Spanish onions, halved and sliced thinly
Salt and ground black pepper

2 cups frozen peas, thawed
6 eggs
2 tsp. chopped fresh mint

Heat the oil in a 9-inch nonstick frying pan. Add the onion, sprinkle with salt, and fry gently for about 25 minutes, until tender. Season to taste, then stir in the peas.

Beat the eggs with the mint, and salt and pepper, then pour them over the onions and peas. Cook gently for about 10 minutes, pulling away the edges of the tortilla as it sets, to allow the uncooked egg to run underneath.

Meanwhile, preheat the broiler. When the tortilla is firm but still moist on top, brown the top under the broiler for about 5 minutes, until golden and set. Allow to cool for a few minutes.

Cover the pan with a plate and carefully invert both pan and plate. Remove the pan. Place another plate on top of the tortilla and invert both plates and tortilla to turn it right-side up. Serve warm or at room temperature, cut into wedges or bite-size pieces.

Serves 8

pinchos

see variations page 146

These salty and piquant little skewers are served with drinks all over Spain. They're the perfect light bite to serve before a big meal.

12 canned or marinated anchovies, drained   12 cornichons
12 caper berries

Roll the anchovies into coils and thread each one onto a separate cocktail stick.

Add a caper berry and cornichon to each stick and serve.

Makes 12

salt cod fritters with garlic mayonnaise

see variations page 147

Salt cod needs to be soaked before cooking, so remember to leave enough time for preparing this recipe. Drain and change the soaking water several times.

Generous 3/4 cup milk
1/2 lb. salt cod, soaked for 24 hours
1 potato (about 1/2 lb.), cooked and mashed
1 shallot, finely chopped
2 tbsp. chopped fresh parsley
Ground black pepper
Juice of 1/2 lemon
2 tbsp. all-purpose flour

1 egg, beaten
1/2 cup dry bread crumbs
Sunflower oil, for frying

for the garlic mayonnaise
1/2 cup mayonnaise
1 1/2 garlic cloves, crushed
1 tsp. lemon juice

Bring the milk to a simmer in a medium pan. Add the cod and poach gently for about 10 minutes, until the fish flakes easily. Remove any skin and bones, and flake the flesh into a bowl. Add the potatoes, shallot, and parsley, and mix well. Season with black pepper and squeeze in lemon juice to taste. Shape the mixture into 8 to 12 patties, dust with flour, dip in beaten egg, then coat in bread crumbs. Place on a platter or tray, cover, and chill for at least 30 minutes. Meanwhile, combine the mayonnaise, garlic, and lemon juice, and add a grind of black pepper. Transfer to a bowl and set aside. Heat about 1 inch sunflower oil in a large pan. Add the patties in batches and fry for about 3 minutes on each side, until golden. Drain on paper towels and serve with the garlic mayonnaise.

Serves 4

garlic spinach with pine nuts

see variations page 148

This classic tapas dish is delicious served with a selection of other dishes to start a meal. Choose simple complementary dishes, such as marinated olives and artichoke hearts, and serve with chunks of crusty bread.

2 tbsp. olive oil
3 tbsp. pine nuts
2 garlic cloves, crushed

9 oz. fresh spinach
Salt and ground black pepper

Heat the oil in a large nonstick saucepan and cook the pine nuts for 2 to 3 minutes, until golden. Add the garlic and cook gently for about 30 seconds.

Add the spinach and cook, tossing and turning the leaves, for about 3 minutes, until wilted. Season with salt and pepper and serve immediately.

Serves 4

spicy fried potatoes & chorizo

see variations page 149

A simple twist on the classic spicy Spanish potatoes, *patatas bravas*, these piping hot potatoes are fabulous to serve with a big jug of sangria. Choose really tiny potatoes if you can, or cut larger ones in half, and provide cocktails sticks for picking them up.

14 oz. new potatoes
3 tbsp. olive oil
7 oz. chorizo, cut into bite-size chunks
2 garlic cloves, crushed

1/2 teaspoon dried chili flakes
Chopped fresh parsley
Salt

Cut any larger potatoes in half to make bite-size pieces. Cook the potatoes in boiling salted water for about 10 minutes, until tender. Drain well, return them to the pan, and leave them off the heat to steam-dry in the heat of the pan.

Heat the oil in a large frying pan. Add the potatoes and fry for about 5 minutes, turning them occasionally. Add the chorizo and continue frying until the potatoes are crisp and golden.

Sprinkle with the garlic and chili, and cook for a further 1 to 2 minutes. Transfer the potatoes to a serving dish. Sprinkle with parsley and a little salt, and serve.

Serves 4

variations

mini meatballs

see base recipe page 127

mini meatballs with roasted bell peppers
Prepare the basic recipe, adding 1 sliced roasted bell pepper with the tomatoes.

mini meatballs with chili
Prepare the basic recipe, adding 1/4 teaspoon dried chili flakes to the sauce.

mini meatballs with thyme
Prepare the basic recipe, using fresh thyme in place of the oregano.

mini meatballs with basil
Prepare the basic recipe, using a small handful of fresh basil in place of the oregano.

mini meatballs with sun-dried tomatoes
Prepare the basic recipe, adding 3 sliced, drained sun-dried tomatoes in oil to the sauce.

variations

broiled mussels

see base recipe page 129

broiled mussels with chives
Prepare the basic recipe, using snipped chives in place of the parsley.

broiled mussels with shallot
Prepare the basic recipe, adding 1 finely chopped shallot to the
topping mixture.

broiled mussels with tarragon
Prepare the basic recipe, using 1 tablespoon chopped fresh tarragon in place
of the parsley.

broiled mussels with cayenne
Prepare the basic recipe, adding a good pinch of cayenne pepper to the
topping mixture in place of black pepper.

variations

garlic & chili shrimp

see base recipe page 130

garlic shrimp
Prepare the basic recipe, omitting the chili and seasoning with ground black
pepper instead.

zesty garlic & chili shrimp
Prepare the basic recipe, sprinkling 1/4 teaspoon grated lemon zest over
the shrimp before serving.

garlic & chili shrimp with parsley
Prepare the basic recipe, sprinkling 1 to 2 tablespoons chopped parsley over
the shrimp before serving.

garlic & chili shrimp with chives
Prepare the basic recipe, sprinkling 1 tablespoon snipped chives over the
shrimp before serving.

green pea tortilla

see base recipe page 133

traditional tortilla
Prepare the basic recipe using 10 1/2 oz. sliced cooked potatoes in place of
the peas, and 1 teaspoon fresh thyme leaves in place of the mint.

green pea tortilla with spicy sausage
Prepare the basic recipe, adding 2 oz. thinly sliced chorizo with the onions.

green pea tortilla with sun-dried tomatoes
Prepare the basic recipe, adding 4 sliced sun-dried tomatoes in oil with
the peas.

fava bean tortilla
Prepare the basic recipe, using lightly cooked fava beans in place of
the peas.

variations

pinchos

see base recipe page 134

simple pinchos
Prepare the basic recipe, omitting the cornichons.

spicy pinchos
Prepare the basic recipe, using pickled chilies in place of the cornichons.

veggie pinchos
Prepare the basic recipe, using strips of roasted bell pepper in place of
the anchovies.

spicy veggie pinchos
Prepare the basic recipe, using strips of roasted bell pepper in place of the
anchovies and pickled chilies in place of the cornichons.

variations

salt cod fritters with garlic mayonnaise

see base recipe page 137

salt cod fritters with lemon mayonnaise
Prepare the basic recipe, adding 1/4 teaspoon grated lemon zest to the
mayonnaise in place of the garlic.

salt cod fritters with herb mayonnaise
Prepare the basic recipe, adding 1 tablespoon snipped fresh chives and
2 teaspoons chopped fresh tarragon to the mayonnaise instead of the garlic.

salt cod fritters with pesto mayonnaise
Prepare the basic recipe, adding 1 tablespoon pesto to the mayonnaise in
place of the garlic and lemon juice.

salt cod fritters with tomato salsa
Prepare the basic recipe, serving the fritters with tomato salsa instead of
the mayonnaise. ·

variations

garlic spinach with pine nuts

see base recipe page 138

garlic spinach with pine nuts & raisins
Prepare the basic recipe, tossing in 2 tablespoons raisins before serving.

garlic spinach with pine nuts & chorizo
Prepare the basic recipe, cooking 2 oz. chopped chorizo with the pine nuts.

garlic spinach with pine nuts & chili
Prepare the basic recipe, adding a good pinch of dried chili flakes with
the spinach.

lemon and garlic spinach with pine nuts
Prepare the basic recipe, adding a good squeeze of lemon juice with
the seasoning.

garlic spinach with pine nuts & dill
Prepare the basic recipe, adding 2 tablespoons chopped fresh dill
before serving.

spicy fried potatoes & chorizo

see base recipe page 141

spicy fried potatoes
Prepare the basic recipe, omitting the chorizo.

spicy fried potatoes with chorizo & marjoram
Prepare the basic recipe, sprinkling the potatoes with 1 teaspoon chopped
fresh marjoram in place of the parsley.

spicy fried potatoes with mayonnaise
Prepare the basic recipe and serve with a dish of garlic mayonnaise
for dunking.

spicy fried potatoes with lemon mayonnaise
Prepare the basic recipe and serve with lemon mayonnaise. Stir 1 teaspoon
grated lemon zest, 2 teaspoons lemon juice, and a good splash of Tabasco
into 1/2 cup mayonnaise.

amazing meze

Traditionally served with drinks, these fabulously
flavored snacks make wonderful appetizers. From
dips and salads to little edible parcels, and skewered
meatballs, there's something for all guests and
occasions in this chapter

feta phyllo pastries

see variations page 167

These crisp, golden pastries are surprisingly easy to make. Serve them with a selection of meze, nestled on a dressed salad, or as a bite-size snack with drinks.

7 oz. feta cheese, crumbled
1 1/2 tbsp. chopped fresh mint
2 eggs, beaten

Ground black pepper
8 sheets phyllo pastry
1/4 cup. (1/2 stick) butter, melted

Preheat the oven to 375°F (190°C). Lightly grease a baking sheet.

Put the feta, mint, and eggs in a bowl, season with pepper, and mix well, mashing the cheese with the eggs.

Lay the phyllo sheets on a board and cut in half lengthwise to make sixteen strips. Take one strip and cover the rest with a damp cloth. Brush the strip with butter and place about 1 tablespoon of the feta mixture at one end, forming it into a sausage shape. Roll the cheese and pastry over once or twice. Fold over the sides of the pastry, and roll up the cheese completely to make a sealed, cigar-shaped pastry. Place on the baking sheet and brush with more butter. Make the remaining pastries in the same way.

Bake the pastries for about 15 minutes, until crisp and golden. Serve hot or transfer to a wire rack and cool, then serve warm or at room temperature.

Makes 16

stuffed grape leaves

see variations page 168

Tender, juicy stuffed grape leaves flavored with fresh mint, scallions, and lemon juice make a great appetizer. Serve them solo, with drinks, or with other meze, such as marinated olives.

1/2 cup rice, cooked
1 bunch scallions, finely sliced
2 tbsp. chopped fresh mint
3 tbsp. olive oil

Juice of 1 lemon
Salt and ground black pepper
20 preserved grape leaves, rinsed
Lemon wedges

Put the rice, scallions, and mint in a bowl. Pour over 1 tablespoon of the oil, add half the lemon juice, and season to taste with salt and pepper. Mix well.

Lay a grape leaf on a board. Place a tablespoon of the rice mixture in a mound near the stalk end. Fold the end over and then fold over the sides. Roll up the rice and leaf into a tight package. Repeat with the remaining leaves and rice. Arrange the rolls in a steamer basket.

Place the steamer basket over a pan of simmering water, drizzle the rolls with the remaining oil, cover, and steam for 40 minutes. (Check the water occasionally, adding more if necessary.)

Transfer the grape leaves to a plate, squeeze a little more lemon juice on them, then allow them to cool. Serve at room temperature, with lemon wedges for squeezing.

Makes 20

baby lettuce leaves filled with tabbouleh

see variations page 169

Tabbouleh is a zesty, herb-flavored salad of nutty bulgur, a part-cooked, cracked wheat product that is ready to eat after soaking (and not to be confused with ordinary cracked wheat, which is raw and has to be boiled). Serve these tabbouleh-filled leaves as a formal appetizer at the table, or as casual finger food with drinks.

1/2 cup bulgur wheat	2 ripe tomatoes, seeded and diced
Salt and ground black pepper	2 tbsp. olive oil
1/3 cup chopped fresh parsley	Juice of 1/2 lemon
1/4 cup chopped fresh mint	12 baby lettuce leaves

Put the bulgur wheat in a bowl, add a good pinch of salt, and pour boiling water over it to cover. Leave to soak for 20 minutes, then drain well.

Combine the bulgur, parsley, mint, and tomato in a large bowl, and season with salt and pepper. Drizzle in the oil, add a squeeze of lemon juice, and toss to combine.

Arrange the lettuce leaves on a serving plate and spoon the tabbouleh into them.

Serves 4

garlicky tomato & eggplant stacks

see variations page 170

These pretty Mediterranean vegetable stacks make a lovely appetizer served at the table. Top each one with a fresh basil leaf, if desired.

1 eggplant
2 tbsp. olive oil, plus extra for brushing
2 garlic cloves, crushed

Salt and ground black pepper
1 lb. cherry tomatoes, halved
Handful of fresh basil leaves, torn

Heat a griddle. Slice the eggplant into twelve 1/2-inch thick rounds, brush with oil on both sides, and season with salt and pepper.

Working in batches, cook the eggplant slices for about 5 minutes on each side, until tender. Transfer to a large dish and keep warm while you cook the remaining slices.

Meanwhile, heat the oil in a medium pan and cook the garlic for about 1 minute. Add the tomatoes and seasoning, and cook gently for about 10 minutes, until soft. Check the seasoning, toss in the basil, and stir to combine.

Arrange the eggplant slices on a platter, top each one with a spoonful of tomatoes, and serve immediately.

Serves 4

falafel with yogurt dip

see variations page 171

Be sure to use dried chickpeas to make these crips fritters and not canned ones, or else the falafel will fall apart during cooking.

1 cup dried chickpeas, soaked in cold water
   overnight
1 onion, finely chopped
1 garlic clove, chopped
1 tsp. ground cumin
1 tsp. ground coriander

Good pinch of cayenne pepper
2 tbsp. chopped fresh parsley
1/2 cup plain yogurt
1 1/2 tbsp. chopped fresh mint
Sunflower oil, for deep-frying
Salt and ground black pepper

Drain the chickpeas and put them in a food processor with the onion, garlic, cumin, coriander, and cayenne pepper. Process to a smooth paste. Season well with salt and pepper, then add the parsley and process briefly to combine.

Rinse your hands under cold water. Take a heaping tablespoon of the mixture and shape it into a patty. Repeat with the remaining mixture, pressing it firmly into shape and wetting your hands to prevent the patties from sticking. Allow to stand for 30 minutes. Meanwhile, combine the yogurt and mint in a serving bowl, season to taste, and chill.

Heat about 1 inch of oil in a frying pan. Working in batches, add the falafel and cook for about 5 minutes, turning once or twice, until crisp and golden all over. Drain on paper towels and keep warm until all are cooked. Serve hot or warm, with the yogurt dip.

Makes about 16, to serve 4

hummus

see variations page 172

This classic dip from the Middle East is delicious served with wedges of pita or vegetable sticks, alone or as part of a meze selection. Tahini is a sesame seed paste.

14-oz. can chickpeas, rinsed and drained
1 garlic clove, crushed
1 tsp. ground cumin
1 tsp. ground coriander

1 tbsp. tahini
3 tbsp. olive oil
Juice of 1/2 to 3/4 lemon
Salt and ground black pepper

Put the chickpeas, garlic, cumin, coriander, tahini, and oil in a food processor and squeeze in the juice of 1/2 lemon.

Process the mixture to a smooth purée, scraping down the sides of the bowl occasionally. Season with salt and pepper, and squeeze in more lemon juice to taste.

Spoon the hummus into a bowl and serve.

Serves 4

lamb koftas

see variations page 173

These lightly spiced lamb skewers make a tasty start to any meal. Serve with a tomato salsa and, if you like, offer a chopped vegetable salad as well.

1/2 lb. lean ground lamb
2 large scallions, finely chopped
1 garlic clove, crushed
1 tsp. ground cumin
1 tsp. ground coriander

1/4 tsp. cayenne pepper
2 tsp. chopped fresh mint
Salt and ground black pepper
Tomato salsa (see page 51), to serve

Soak 8 wooden toothpicks in cold water for 15 minutes.

In a bowl, mix the lamb, scallions, garlic, cumin, coriander, cayenne and mint until combined. Season well with salt and pepper. Use your hands to mix the ingredients thoroughly.

Divide the meat into 8 pieces, and shape them into small egg-shaped balls. Thread each ball onto a toothpick and press it out to form a sausage shape. Chill for about 30 minutes.

Preheat the broiler. Broil the skewers for 5 to 8 minutes, turning once or twice, until cooked through. Serve with tomato salsa.

Serves 4

grilled halloumi with garlic, lemon & chili

see variations page 174

This wonderful salty cheese is traditionally served grilled or fried, when it softens to a deliciously chewy texture. You can find it in most supermarkets and Mediterranean food stores.

7 oz. halloumi
1 garlic clove, crushed
1/4 tsp. dried chili flakes

Juice of 1 lemon
2 tbsp. olive oil

Slice the cheese into 1/4-inch thick slices and arrange in a large dish.

Whisk together the garlic, chili, lemon juice, and oil, and pour over the cheese, turning the slices to coat them. Allow to marinate for at least 1 hour.

Heat a dry, nonstick frying pan or griddle. Cook the cheese for 1 to 2 minutes on each side, until golden and sizzling. Serve immediately, as the cheese will toughen on cooling.

Serves 4

spiced carrot salad

see variations page 175

With its fiery color, this simple carrot salad looks stunning, and it makes a deliciously light start to any meal.

1 lb. carrots, finely sliced
Salt
1 small garlic clove, crushed
1/4 tsp. ground ginger
1/2 tsp. ground cumin
1/4 tsp. ground coriander

1/4 tsp. paprika
Good pinch of cayenne pepper
2 tsp. red wine vinegar
1 1/2 tbsp. olive oil
1 tsp. chopped fresh mint, plus extra for
    sprinkling

Put the carrots in a medium saucepan with 2 tablespoon water, season with salt, cover tightly, then cook over a low heat, shaking the pan now and again, for about 10 minutes, until tender. Remove the lid and cook the carrots, uncovered, for a minute or two until all the liquid has evaporated. Remove from the heat.

Whisk together the garlic, ginger, cumin, coriander, paprika, cayenne, vinegar, and oil, and season with salt. Stir in the mint, then pour the mixture over the carrots in the pan. Let stand for at least 30 minutes.

To serve, warm the carrots for a few seconds over low heat, if necessary, or serve them at room temperature, sprinkled with a little extra mint.

Serves 4

variations

feta phyllo pastries

see base recipe page 151

feta phyllo pastries with pine nuts
Prepare the basic recipe, adding 1 tablespoon toasted pine nuts to the
feta mixture.

feta & spinach phyllo pastries
Prepare the basic mixture, stirring in 3 tablespoons thawed, drained, and
chopped spinach when the feta has combined with the eggs.

feta & herb phyllo pastries
Prepare the basic recipe, adding 2 teaspoons snipped fresh chives and
2 tablespoons chopped fresh parsley to the feta mixture.

feta & scallion phyllo pastries
Prepare the basic recipe, adding 1 bunch finely sliced scallions to the feta
mixture.

variations

stuffed grape leaves

see base recipe page 153

stuffed grape leaves with dill
Prepare the basic recipe, adding 2 teaspoon chopped fresh dill to the rice mixture.

spicy stuffed grape leaves
Prepare the basic recipe, adding a good pinch of cayenne pepper to the rice mixture.

stuffed grape leaves with pine nuts
Prepare the basic recipe, adding 1 tablespoon toasted pine nuts to the rice mixture.

stuffed grape leaves with red onion
Prepare the basic recipe, adding 1 small finely chopped red onion to the rice mixture.

variations

baby lettuce leaves filled with tabbouleh

see base recipe page 154

tabbouleh with cucumber
Prepare the basic recipe, adding 1/4 diced, seeded cucumber with
the tomato.

tabbouleh with scallions
Prepare the basic recipe, adding 4 thinly sliced scallions with
the tomato.

tabbouleh with cilantro
Prepare the basic recipe, adding 1/3 cup chopped fresh cilantro
in place of the mint.

tabbouleh with green chili
Prepare the basic recipe, adding 1 finely chopped, seeded fresh green
chili with the tomato.

spiced tabbouleh
Prepare the basic recipe, adding 1/4 teaspoon ground cumin and
1/4 teaspoon ground coriander with the tomato.

variations

garlicky tomato & eggplant stacks

see base recipe page 157

spicy tomato & eggplant stacks
Prepare the basic recipe, adding 1/2 teaspoon dried chili flakes to
the tomatoes.

garlicky tomato, eggplant & olive stacks
Prepare the basic recipe, adding 10 halved pitted black olives to
the tomatoes.

garlicky tomato & eggplant stacks with feta
Prepare the basic recipe, topping the tomato stacks with crumbled feta.

garlicky tomato & eggplant stacks with Parmesan
Prepare the basic recipe, topping the tomato stacks with shavings of
Parmesan cheese.

garlicky tomato & eggplant stacks with oregano
Prepare the basic recipe, adding 1 teaspoon fresh oregano leaves with the
tomatoes. Omit the basil.

falafel with yogurt dip

see base recipe page 158

spicy falafel with yogurt dip
Prepare the basic recipe, adding 1/4 teaspoon dried chili flakes in place of the cayenne pepper.

falafel in pita pockets
Prepare the basic recipe and serve the falafel in split, warmed pita breads, with chopped tomato and cucumber, and drizzled with yogurt dressing.

falafel with tomato salsa
Prepare the basic recipe and serve with tomato salsa instead of the yogurt dip.

falafel with cucumber & yogurt dip
Prepare the basic recipe, adding 1/4 grated, seeded cucumber to the yogurt dip.

falafel with fresh salad
Prepare the basic recipe and serve the falafel and dip with a crunchy lettuce, cucumber, and tomato salad.

variations

hummus

see base recipe page 161

avocado hummus
Prepare the basic recipe, adding 1 small peeled and pitted avocado.

roasted bell pepper hummus
Preheat the oven to 450°F (230°C). Place 1 red bell pepper on a baking sheet and bake for about 30 minutes, until blackened. Put the pepper in a bowl, cover with plastic wrap, and leave to stand for about 10 minutes. Peel and seed, then cut the flesh into chunks. Prepare the basic recipe, adding the red pepper chunks before processing.

hummus with sesame seeds
Prepare the basic recipe, adding 1 tablespoon sesame seeds in place of the tahini.

hummus with dill
Prepare the basic recipe, sprinkling the hummus with chopped fresh dill before serving.

spicy hummus
Prepare the basic recipe, adding 1/2 teaspoon dried chili flakes.

variations

lamb koftas

see base recipe page 162

lamb kofta wraps
Serve the koftas and tomato salsa wrapped in quartered flour tortillas.

beef koftas
Prepare the basic recipe, using ground beef instead of lamb.

chicken or turkey koftas
Prepare the basic recipe, using ground chicken or turkey instead of lamb.

harissa-spiced lamb koftas
Prepare the basic recipe, using 1 to 2 teaspoons harissa (hot chili paste)
in place of the cumin, coriander, and cayenne.

lemon lamb koftas
Prepare the basic recipe, adding the grated zest of 1/2 lemon with
the spices.

grilled halloumi with garlic, lemon & chili

see base recipe page 165

grilled halloumi with lemon & chili
Prepare the basic recipe, omitting the garlic.

grilled halloumi with garlic, lemon & oregano
Prepare the basic recipe, adding 1 teaspoon fresh oregano leaves in place of the chili.

grilled halloumi with garlic & lemon
Prepare the basic recipe, omitting the chili.

grilled halloumi with garlic, lemon & cumin
Prepare the basic recipe, adding 1/2 teaspoon crushed cumin seeds in place of the chili.

grilled halloumi with fennel, lemon & chili
Prepare the basic recipe, adding 1/2 teaspoon crushed fennel seeds in place of the garlic.

spiced carrot salad

see base recipe page 166

carrot salad with harissa
Prepare the basic recipe, using 1 teaspoon harissa (hot chili paste) in place
of the paprika and cayenne pepper.

spiced beet salad
Prepare the basic recipe, using cooked beets in place of the carrots. Thinly
slice the cooked beets, then simply add the dressing and serve at room
temperature.

spiced fava bean salad
Prepare the basic recipe, using fava beans instead of carrots. Cook the
beans in a pan of boiling water for about 3 minutes, until tender, then
drain and dress.

carrot salad with cilantro
Prepare the basic recipe, using 1 tablespoon chopped fresh cilantro
in place of the mint, and sprinkling with more cilantro to serve.

asian flavor

A classic Asian meal doesn't start with appetizers, but the fabulous array of snacks that are served at other times of day are perfect before a meal. Serve as cocktail snacks or sit down and enjoy them at the table. For a unique dinner party twist, involve your guests in preparing sushi rolls or duck wraps.

thai crab cakes with chili vinegar

see variations page 193

These spicy little fish cakes are perfect to start a Southeast-Asian-style meal, but they also make a great snack to serve with cocktails.

Two 6-oz. cans crabmeat, drained
2 tsp. red curry paste
1 tsp. grated fresh ginger
2 tbsp. chopped cilantro
1/2 tsp. Thai fish sauce
1 egg
2 tbsp. all-purpose flour
Sunflower oil, for frying

for the chili vinegar
1 tbsp. sugar
1/4 cup rice wine vinegar
2 tsp. Thai fish sauce
2 fresh red chilies, seeded and sliced

Prepare the chili vinegar: warm the sugar, vinegar, and fish sauce in a small pan, stirring until the sugar has dissolved. Pour into a small bowl, add the chilies, and set aside to cool.

Put the crabmeat, curry paste, ginger, coriander, and fish sauce in a medium bowl, and mix together well using a fork. Stir in the egg, then sprinkle in the flour and mix well to combine. Shape the mixture into 16 small fish cakes.

Heat about 1 tablespoon oil in a nonstick frying pan. Fry the fish cakes in batches if necessary for 2 to 3 minutes on each side, until golden. Drain well on paper towels and serve hot, with chili vinegar for dipping.

Makes 16

chicken satay with spicy peanut sauce

see variations page 194

These Indonesian-style skewers are a great way to start a barbecue, and they're equally good cooked and eaten indoors — either at the table, or as a pre-dinner nibble.

3 skinless, boneless chicken breasts
1 garlic clove, crushed
1 tsp. grated fresh ginger
Grated zest and juice of 1 lime
1 tsp. Thai fish sauce

for the peanut sauce
2 tbsp. coconut milk
4 tbsp. crunchy peanut butter
Juice of 1/2 lime
1/4 tsp. dried chili flakes

Slice each chicken breast into 4 long strips. Combine the garlic, ginger, lime zest and juice, and fish sauce, and pour over the chicken. Cover and marinate for about 1 hour. Meanwhile, soak 12 bamboo skewers in cold water.

Preheat the broiler. Thread a strip of chicken onto each skewer. Cook the chicken for about 3 minutes on each side, until cooked through.

Meanwhile, stir the coconut milk into the peanut butter until smooth and creamy. Stir in the lime juice and chili. Serve immediately with the chicken satay.

Makes 12

salt & pepper squid

see variations page 195

Crisp and tender, deep-fried squid makes a fabulous start to any meal. If you're serving the squid with drinks, offer toothpicks to pick up the squid rings.

1 lb. squid, cleaned
Juice of 2 limes
1/2 tsp. coarse sea salt
1 tbsp. ground black pepper

1/3 cup rice flour
Sunflower oil, for deep-frying
Lime wedges and sweet chili sauce, to serve

Pull the head and tentacles from the squid bodies. Discard the plastic-like quills running down inside the body sacs, and slice the bodies into rings. Add a squeeze of the lime juice, toss to combine, then marinate in the refrigerator for about 15 minutes.

Meanwhile, combine the salt, pepper, and rice flour. Drain the squid and pat dry on paper towels, then toss the rings in the rice flour mixture.

Fill a deep pan by one-third with the oil and heat to 350°F (180°C), or until a cube of bread browns in about 1 minute.

Working in batches, deep-fry the squid for about 1 minute, until crisp and golden. Drain well on paper towels and serve with lime wedges and sweet chili sauce for dipping.

Serves 4

fruity lamb samosas

see variations page 196

Indian samosas are traditionally deep-fried, but this healthier version is made with phyllo pastry and baked.

2 tbsp. sunflower oil
1 small onion
2 garlic cloves, crushed
1 1/2 tsp. ground cumin
1 1/2 tsp. ground coriander
1/4 tsp. cayenne pepper

1/2 lb. ground lamb
2 tsp. mango chutney, plus extra to serve
Salt and ground black pepper
12 sheets phyllo pastry
3 1/2 tbsp. butter, melted

Preheat the oven to 400°F (200°C). Lightly grease a baking sheet. Heat the oil in a nonstick pan and gently cook the onion and garlic for about 4 minutes. Stir in the spices. Add the lamb and fry, stirring, for 2 to 3 minutes until browned all over. Drain off excess fat, then stir in the mango chutney and season to taste.

Lay a sheet of pastry on a board, brush with butter, and fold over lengthwise to make a long, double-thick strip. Brush with more butter. Place a heaping spoonful of the lamb mixture in the bottom corner of the pastry. Fold the pastry and filling over to enclose it in a triangle. Continue folding the triangle from corner to corner to make a sealed, triangular pastry. Repeat to make another 11 samosas. Place the samosas on a baking sheet and bake for 15 to 20 minutes, until crisp and golden. Serve with mango chutney for dunking.

Makes 12

sushi rolls

see variations page 197

Traditional sushi is made with a special Japanese short-grained rice, but it can work just as well with sticky jasmine rice, which is more readily available in supermarkets.

1 cup jasmine or basmati rice
2 tbsp. rice vinegar
1 1/2 tsp. sugar
1/2 tsp. salt
3 nori sheets
Soy sauce and pickled ginger, to serve

for the filling
1 tbsp. mayonnaise
1/4 tsp. wasabi paste
3 oz. canned crabmeat
1/4 cucumber, seeded and cut into matchstick
    strips

Put the rice in a saucepan and pour in 2 1/2 cups boiling water. Return to a boil, reduce the heat, cover, and simmer for 12 minutes, until the water is absorbed. Remove from the heat and keep covered, for 10 minutes. Meanwhile, mix together the vinegar, sugar, and salt. Turn the rice into a bowl and fold the vinegar dressing into it, then leave to cool to room temperature. Combine the mayonnaise and wasabi, then fold in the crabmeat. Cut the nori in half lengthwise to make six sheets. Lay a sheet of nori on a bamboo rolling mat and place a line of rice along one long edge. Spread a little crab mixture and a line of cucumber sticks on the rice. Using the rolling mat, roll up the nori tightly to enclose the filling. Use a sharp knife to slice the roll into 6 smaller sushi rolls. Rinse and wipe the knife between cuts, if it becomes sticky. Repeat with the remaining nori sheets, crab, and cucumber. Serve on a platter, with soy sauce for dipping and pickled ginger.

Makes 36

vietnamese crystal rolls

see variations page 198

These rolls are fabulous for whetting the appetite, and they are low fat, too. For a fun do-it-yourself appetizer, place all the ingredients in bowls so that guests can assemble the rolls themselves.

12 Vietnamese rice paper wrappers
2 handfuls bean sprouts
1 carrot, cut into matchstick strips
1/2 cucumber, seeded and cut into matchstick strips
4 oz. firm tofu, cut into small cubes

3 scallions, thinly sliced
2 garlic cloves, finely chopped
1/4 cup peanuts, chopped
Soy sauce and sweet chili sauce, for drizzling
Handful of cilantro

Fill a large, shallow bowl with water. Dip a rice paper wrapper in the water for about 20 seconds, until softened. Lay it on a plate.

Sprinkle bean sprouts down the middle of the wrapper. Sprinkle carrot, cucumber, tofu, scallions, garlic, and peanuts on top. Drizzle over a little soy sauce and sweet chili sauce, and sprinkle on a few coriander leaves.

Fold the short ends of the wrapper over to enclose the filling, then roll up tightly to make a sealed parcel. Repeat with the remaining wrappers and filling, and serve immediately.

Makes 12

peking duck wraps

see variations page 199

These mini duck wraps make a really pretty appetizer, either as finger food with drinks or arranged on a plate with a few salad leaves.

2 boneless duck breasts
Salt
12 Chinese pancakes, halved
2 tbsp. hoisin sauce
6 scallions, shredded
1/4 cucumber, seeded, cut into matchstick strips

for the marinade
1 tbsp. soy sauce
1 tbsp. honey
1/2 tsp. Chinese five-spice powder

Score the fat on the duck breasts in a lattice pattern and rub with salt. For the marinade, mix the soy sauce, honey, and five-spice powder, and spoon this over the flesh side of the duck. Marinate in the fridge for at least 1 hour.

Remove the duck from the marinade and pat dry. Heat a nonstick pan. Place the duck in the pan, fat side down. Cook for about 10 minutes, then pour off most of the fat and turn over. Fry for 5 more minutes, until cooked through. Transfer to a board and let rest for 5 minutes.

Meanwhile, spread each pancake with a thin layer of hoisin sauce. Slice the duck thinly, then place several slices on each pancake, top with a little scallion and a few sticks of cucumber and fold the pancake into a cone. Repeat with the remaining pancakes, duck, scallions, and cucumber, and serve.

Serves 4

sticky glazed pork ribs

see variations page 200

Serve these sticky ribs to chew on with drinks or arrange them on a salad for a sit-down appetizer. Either way, be sure you offer plenty of napkins for wiping sticky fingers.

3 tbsp. honey
1 tsp. soy sauce
2 tsp. Chinese five-spice powder

Ground black pepper
12 pork ribs

Preheat the oven to 400°F (200°C).

Combine the honey, soy sauce, and five-spice powder, and season with black pepper in a large bowl. Add the ribs and turn them to coat them all over in the honey mixture.

Put the ribs in a roasting pan in a single layer, brush remaining glaze over them, and bake for 30 minutes, until glossy and well browned. Serve hot.

Serves 4

pea & potato pakora with yogurt

see variations page 201

These crisp and spicy little battered bites are delicious with plain yogurt for dunking.
Serve them as a snack with drinks, or with a selection of Asian-style dips and relishes.

1 lb. potatoes, boiled and mashed
1 cup frozen peas, thawed
2–3 fresh green chilies, seeded and finely
   chopped
4 scallions, finely sliced
2 tsp. ground cumin
1 tsp. ground coriander
3 tbsp. chopped cilantro

Salt
1 cup gram flour (chickpea flour or besan)
1 tsp. ground turmeric
1/2 tsp. chili powder
1 tsp. baking powder
Generous 3/4 cup cold water
Sunflower oil, for deep-frying
Plain yogurt, to serve

Mix the potatoes, peas, chilies, scallions, ground cumin, coriander, and cilantro in a bowl.
Season with salt and stir well. Shape the mixture into 16 walnut-sized balls, place on a
platter and chill for at least 30 minutes, until firm. Mix the gram flour, turmeric, chili powder,
and baking powder in a bowl. Pour in about one-fourth of the water and stir with a fork
until a thick, smooth paste forms. Stir in the remaining water to make a smooth batter.

Pour oil into a pan until it is one-third full and heat to 350°F (180°C), or until a cube of
bread browns in about 1 minute. Working in batches, dip the potato balls into the batter and
fry them for about 2 minutes, until golden and crisp. Remove with a slotted spoon and drain
on paper towels. Keep hot until all are cooked. Serve hot with yogurt for dipping.

Serves 4

variations

thai crab cakes with chili vinegar

see base recipe page 177

green curry crab cakes with chili vinegar
Prepare the basic recipe, using green curry paste in place of the red
curry paste.

thai crab cakes with lemongrass and chili vinegar
Finely chop the fleshy bulb of 1 lemongrass stalk. Prepare the basic recipe,
adding the chopped lemongrass to the crab cake mixture.

zesty thai crab cakes with chili vinegar
Prepare the basic recipe, adding the grated zest of 1 lime to the crab
cake mixture.

thai crab cakes with sweet chili sauce
Prepare the basic recipe and serve the crab cakes with sweet chili sauce in
place of the chili vinegar.

variations

chicken satay with spicy peanut sauce

see base recipe page 179

pork satay
Prepare the basic recipe, using strips of pork loin in place of the chicken.

beef satay
Prepare the basic recipe, using strips of beef fillet in place of the chicken.

tofu satay
Prepare the basic recipe, using fingers of firm tofu in place of the chicken.

shrimp satay
Prepare the basic recipe, using peeled raw tiger shrimp in place of the chicken. Allow 2 shrimp per skewer.

salt & pepper squid

see base recipe page 180

hot chili squid
Prepare the basic recipe, using 1 teaspoon dried chili flakes in place of
the black pepper.

spiced salt & pepper squid
Prepare the basic recipe, adding 1 teaspoon ground cumin to the
salt-and-pepper mixture.

salt & pepper squid with cilantro
Prepare the basic recipe, sprinkling the fried squid with chopped fresh
cilantro before serving.

salt & pepper squid with lemon
Prepare the basic recipe, using lemons in place of the limes.

variations

fruity lamb samosas

see base recipe page 183

spicy beef samosas
Prepare the basic recipe, using ground beef in place of the lamb, and omitting the mango chutney.

spicy chicken samosas
Prepare the basic recipe, using ground chicken in place of the lamb.

spicy pork samosas
Prepare the basic recipe, using ground pork in place of the lamb.

spicy lamb & pea samosas
Prepare the basic recipe, adding 1/2 cup thawed frozen peas to the lamb mixture.

fruity lamb samosas with cilantro
Prepare the basic recipe, adding 3 tablespoons chopped fresh cilantro to the lamb mixture.

variations

sushi rolls

see base recipe page 184

roasted bell pepper & crab sushi rolls
Prepare the basic recipe, using strips of roasted bell pepper in place of the cucumber strips.

avocado & smoked salmon sushi rolls
Prepare the basic recipe, using strips of smoked salmon and mashed avocado in place of the crab mix and cucumber.

egg-cup sushi
Prepare the basic recipe for sushi rice. Line an egg cup with plastic wrap, then press a thin slice of smoked salmon in it. Fill with rice, then turn out. Repeat to make more sushi molds.

tuna & cucumber sushi rolls
Prepare the basic recipe, using tuna in place of the crab meat.

roasted bell pepper & avocado sushi rolls
Prepare the basic recipe, using mashed avocado spiked with wasabi in place of the crab, and strips of roasted bell red pepper in place of the cucumber.

vietnamese crystal rolls

see base recipe page 187

vietnamese crystal rolls with avocado
Finely dice the flesh of 1 avocado and sprinkle over the bean sprouts with the other filling ingredients.

vietnamese crystal rolls with sweet bell pepper
Finely dice 1 red or yellow bell pepper and sprinkle over the bean sprouts with the other filling ingredients.

vietnamese crystal rolls with chicken
Skin and dice 1 cooked boneless chicken breast and use in place of the tofu.

vietnamese crystal rolls with basil
Prepare the basic recipe, using chopped fresh basil in place of the cilantro.

vietnamese crystal rolls with mint
Prepare the basic recipe, using chopped fresh mint in place of the cilantro.

variations

peking duck wraps

see base recipe page 188

sweet & spicy duck wraps
Prepare the basic recipe, spreading the pancakes with sweet chili sauce
instead of hoisin sauce.

duck wraps with fresh mango
Cut the flesh of 1/2 peeled and pitted mango into matchstick strips.
Prepare the basic recipe, adding a few sticks of mango to each wrap.

gingered duck wraps
Prepare the basic recipe, adding 1 teaspoon grated fresh root ginger to the
duck marinade.

garlic-marinated duck wraps
Prepare the basic recipe, stirring 1 crushed garlic clove into the marinade.

duck wraps with bean sprouts
Prepare the basic recipe, adding a few bean sprouts to each filled pancake
before rolling up.

variations

sticky glazed pork ribs

see base recipe page 191

spicy glazed pork ribs
Prepare the basic recipe, adding 1/4 teaspoon crushed dried chili to the honey and soy mixture.

sticky glazed pork ribs with ginger
Prepare the basic recipe, adding 1 teaspoon grated fresh root ginger to the honey and soy mixture.

sticky glazed pork ribs with cinnamon
Prepare the basic recipe, adding 1 teaspoon cinnamon to the honey and soy mixture.

sticky glazed pork ribs with cumin
Prepare the basic recipe, adding 1 teaspoon ground cumin to the honey and soy mixture.

pea & potato pakora with yogurt

see base recipe page 192

pea & potato pakora with tomato & onion salad
Finely slice 1 red onion and dice 4 seeded tomatoes. Season with salt and
pepper, add the juice of 1 lime, and serve with the pakora.

minty pea & potato pakoras with yogurt
Prepare the basic recipe, using 1 1/2 tablespoons chopped fresh mint in
place of the cilantro.

pea & potato pakora with mango chutney
Prepare the basic recipe and serve with mango chutney.

pea & potato pakora with minted yogurt
Stir 3 tablespoons chopped fresh mint into 1 cup plain yogurt and season
with a pinch of salt and a pinch of cayenne pepper. Serve with the pakora.

quick canapés & hors d'oeuvres

These elegant starters are fast, easy, and delicious.
Less time in the kitchen means more time to be
with your guests, but no one will think you've
scrimped on time when you produce a platter of
these elegant bites.

hummus & roasted bell pepper mini wraps

see variations page 219

You can rustle up these pretty tortilla pinwheels in less than 10 minutes — making them the perfect choice for instant entertaining.

2 soft flour tortillas
6 tbsp. hummus

2 bottled roasted bell red peppers
Ground black pepper

Lay the tortillas on a board and spread each one with 3 tablespoons hummus.

Pat the peppers dry on a paper towel, then cut into strips and scatter over the tortillas. Season with black pepper and roll up the tortillas tightly. Trim off the ends of each roll and slice each roll into six pieces. Arrange the mini wraps on a serving plate.

Makes 12

mini blinis with horseradish cream & caviar

see variations page 220

You can buy packets of blinis from most good supermarkets. Serve them cold if you want to prepare these canapés ahead, but they're even better warm.

12 mini blinis
6 tbsp. crème fraîche or sour cream
3/4 tsp. grated lemon zest

3/4 tsp. creamed horseradish
1–2 tbsp. caviar
Snipped fresh chives, for sprinkling (optional)

Preheat the oven according to the package instructions for heating the blini. Combine the crème fraîche or sour cream with the lemon zest and horseradish and set aside.

Place the blinis on a baking sheet and warm through for about 5 minutes or according to the package instructions. Arrange the blinis on a serving platter.

Top each blini with a spoonful of the crème fraîche or sour cream mixture and about 1/4 teaspoon caviar. Sprinkle with snipped chives, if desired, and serve.

Makes 12

mashed pea & ham crostini

see variations page 221

Buy a very elegant, narrow baguette to make these crostini. If you can find only larger baguettes, cut the slices in half to make bite-size toasts.

2 shallots, finely chopped
2 tbsp. olive oil, plus extra for drizzling
1 cup frozen peas
2 tbsp. white wine
3 strips prosciutto

12 thin baguette slices
1 garlic clove, halved
Chopped fresh mint, for sprinkling
Salt and ground black pepper

Gently cook the shallots in the oil for about 3 minutes, until slightly softened. Add the peas and wine, cover, and cook gently for about 4 minutes, until the peas are tender.

Meanwhile, cut each strip of prosciutto in half widthwise, then slice across to make twelve strips. Put the peas and juices in a food processor, season with salt and pepper, and process to make a chunky purée.

Toast the bread on both sides until golden. Rub one side of each toast with the cut side of the garlic clove, then spoon mashed peas on top and finish with a twist of ham. Drizzle with a little more oil, if desired, and a grinding of black pepper.

Sprinkle the crostini with mint and serve immediately.

Makes 12

mini poppadums with onion relish

see variations page 222

These thin, deep-fried Indian crispbreads are great with cocktails. For a more informal approach, serve the relish in a bowl and the poppadums for scooping.

1 red onion, quartered and thinly sliced
1/4 cucumber, halved, seeded, and sliced
1 green chili, seeded and finely chopped
1/4 tsp. ground coriander
Handful of fresh cilantro, chopped

Pinch of sugar
Salt and ground black pepper
Juice of 1 lime
16 mini poppadums

Put the onion, cucumber, and chili in a bowl. Sprinkle over the coriander, cilantro, and sugar, and season with salt, then add a squeeze of lime juice. Toss to combine.

Arrange the mini poppadums on a plate and fill each one with a spoonful of the onion relish. Serve immediately.

Makes 16

pesto & artichoke bruschetta

see variations page 223

Nothing could be simpler than these bruschetta. There are all kinds of charbroiled, marinated artichokes available, so select the type you prefer.

2 tbsp. pesto
2 tbsp. crème fraîche
12 thin baguette slices
Small jar of chargrilled artichoke hearts,
    drained (12 pieces)

12 fresh basil leaves
Ground black pepper

Combine the pesto and crème fraîche, then set aside.

Toast the bread until golden on both sides. Spread each toast with pesto mixture, top with a piece of artichoke heart, and add a fresh basil leaf. Season with black pepper and serve freshly prepared.

Makes 12

walnut toasts with warm goats cheese & fig

see variations page 224

Tart, piquant goats cheese and sweet juicy fig are a natural partnership for a simple, elegant canapé on rich walnut toast. Any other good bread can be used instead of walnut bread if desired.

4 slices walnut bread
4 oz. goats cheese

2 tbsp. toasted pine nuts
2 figs, each cut into 6 wedges

Preheat the broiler. Cut each slice of bread into three bite-size pieces and toast on one side.

Meanwhile, slice the goats cheese and into 12 bite-size pieces. Turn the toasts, uncooked sides up. Top each toast with a piece of cheese and broil for about 2 minutes, until golden and bubbling.

Sprinkle the pine nuts over the toasts, top with a wedge of fig, and serve immediately.

Makes 12

pumpernickel with sour cream & beet caviar

see variations page 225

The distinctive taste of dark brown pumpernickel is sublime with sour cream and sweet, juicy beets in these Eastern-European-style canapés.

1 tsp. balsamic vinegar
1 tsp. olive oil
1/4-1/2 tsp. whole-grain mustard
2 cooked beets, finely diced

4 slices pumpernickel
1/2 cup sour cream
Snipped fresh chives, to garnish

Mix the vinegar, oil, and mustard in a large bowl. Add the beets and toss until coated.

Cut each slice of pumpernickel into four squares and arrange them on a serving platter. Top each slice with a dollop of sour cream, a spoonful of beets, and a sprinkling of chives. Serve freshly prepared.

Serves 4

smoked mackerel pâté on finger toasts

see variations page 226

As a snack with drinks, this quick appetizer couldn't be simpler, and it can be served with salad as a more formal starter. Leftover pâté can be stored in a covered container in the refrigerator for 3 to 4 days.

7 oz. smoked mackerel fillets, skinned
1/2 cup Greek yogurt
Ground black pepper

Juice of 1/4 to 1/2 lemon
4 slices whole wheat bread
Chopped fresh parsley

Put the fish and yogurt in a food processor, season with black pepper, and process to a smooth paste. Stir in lemon juice to taste.

Remove the crusts from the bread, then toast the slices on both sides. Slice each toast into 3 fingers, spread with pâté, sprinkle with chopped fresh parsley, and serve.

Serves 4

crostini with blue cheese & pear

see variations page 227

Sharp, salty blue cheese and sweet, juicy pear make a sublime combination on these crunchy little toasts. Creamy gorgonzola is particularly good, but any blue cheese will do.

1 pear	2 3/4 oz. gorgonzola cheese, thinly sliced
12 thin baguette slices	Freshly ground black pepper

Peel and core the pear, then slice it into 12 thin wedges.

Toast the bread until golden on both sides. Top each toast with a sliver of blue cheese, a wedge of pear, and a good grinding of black pepper. Serve immediately.

Makes 12

hummus & roasted bell pepper mini wraps

see base recipe page 203

hummus, roasted bell pepper & basil mini wraps
Prepare the basic recipe, scattering a few fresh basil leaves over the peppers before rolling up and slicing.

hummus, roasted bell pepper & sweet chili mini wraps
Prepare the basic recipe, drizzling 1 teaspoon sweet chili sauce over each hummus-spread wrap before scattering over the peppers and rolling up.

cream cheese & roasted red bell pepper mini wraps
Prepare the basic recipe, using cream cheese in place of the hummus.

cream cheese & smoked salmon mini wraps
Cut 2 oz. smoked salmon into strips. Prepare the basic recipe using cream cheese in place of the hummus, and scattering the wraps with the smoked salmon in place of the red pepper.

hummus, carrot & cilantro mini wraps
Peel and grate 1 carrot and chop a handful of fresh cilantro. Prepare the basic recipe, scattering grated carrot over the hummus in place of the red pepper, and sprinkling with cilantro before rolling up.

variations

mini blinis with horseradish cream & caviar

see base recipe page 205

mini blinis with horseradish cream & roasted bell pepper strips
Prepare the basic recipe, using strips of bottled roasted bell peppers in place of the caviar.

mini blinis with horseradish cream & salami twists
Prepare the basic recipe, using strips of salami in place of the caviar.

mini blinis with horseradish cream & smoked trout
Gently break a smoked trout fillet into 12 flakes, removing any bones. Prepare the basic recipe, using the smoked trout in place of the caviar.

mini blinis with horseradish cream & smoked salmon
Prepare the basic recipe, topping each blini with a strip of smoked salmon in place of the caviar.

mini blinis with smoked salmon & caviar
Prepare the basic recipe, topping each blini with a strip of smoked salmon and a dollop of caviar.

mashed pea & ham crostini

see base recipe page 206

mashed pea & Parmesan crostini
Prepare the basic recipe, topping each crostini with shavings of Parmesan cheese in place of the prosciutto.

mashed pea & smoked trout crostini
Gently break a smoked trout fillet into 12 large flakes. Prepare the basic recipe, topping each crostini with a piece of smoked trout in place of the prosciutto.

mashed pea & cherry tomato crostini
Cut 12 cherry tomatoes in half. Prepare the basic recipe, topping each crostini with 2 cherry tomato halves in place of the prosciutto.

mashed pea & chorizo crostini
Prepare the basic recipe, using 12 slices of wafer-thin chorizo in place of the prosciutto.

mashed pea crostini with sun-dried tomatoes
Drain 4 sun-dried tomatoes in oil, then slice thinly. Prepare the basic recipe, topping the crostini with strips of sun-dried tomato in place of the prosciutto.

variations

mini poppadums with onion relish

see base recipe page 209

mini poppadums with onion & tomato relish
Prepare the basic recipe, adding 1 finely chopped, seeded tomato to the relish.

mini poppadums with onion & mango relish
Prepare the basic recipe, adding 1/2 small chopped, peeled, and pitted mango to the relish in place of the cucumber.

mini poppadums with onion & coconut relish
Prepare the basic recipe, adding 2 tablespoons grated fresh coconut to the relish.

mini poppadums with onion relish & mango chutney
Prepare the basic recipe, adding a dollop of mango chutney to each filled poppadum.

pesto & artichoke bruschetta

see base recipe page 210

garlic & artichoke bruschetta
Halve a garlic clove. Prepare the basic recipe, rubbing the toasts with garlic and drizzling with a little extra virgin olive oil instead of spreading with pesto.

pesto & artichoke bruschetta with arugula
Prepare the basic recipe, adding a few arugula leaves to each bruschetta in place of the basil leaves.

pesto & artichoke bruschetta with olives
Prepare the basic recipe, adding a pitted black or stuffed green olive to each bruschetta.

pesto & artichoke bruschetta with pecorino
Prepare the basic recipe, adding a few shavings of Pecorino cheese to each bruschetta.

pesto & cherry tomato bruschetta
Prepare the basic recipe, topping each toast with 3 cherry tomato halves.

walnut toasts with warm goats cheese & fig

see base recipe page 213

bruschetta with warm goats cheese & fig
Prepare the basic recipe, using 12 baguette slices in place of the walnut bread. Toast on both sides until golden, then simply top with the cheese, a wedge of fig, and a grinding of black pepper.

walnut toasts with warm goats cheese & chili jam
Prepare the basic recipe, spreading the toast with chili jam before topping with goats cheese.

walnut toasts with warm goats cheese & peach
Prepare the basic recipe, using a ripe peach cut into slim wedges in place of the figs.

walnut toasts with warm goats cheese & honey
Prepare the basic recipe, drizzling the goats cheese with a little honey before broiling.

pumpernickel with sour cream & beet caviar

see base recipe page 214

pumpernickel with sour cream & caviar
Prepare the basic recipe, topping each canapé with a teaspoonful of caviar in place of the dressed beets.

pumpernickel with sour cream & char-grilled artichokes
Drain a bottle of marinated artichoke hearts and cut in half. Prepare the basic recipe, using the artichokes in place of the dressed beets. Sprinkle with a little grated lemon zest and a grinding of black pepper before serving.

pumpernickel with sour cream & smoked salmon
Cut 1 to 2 slices of smoked salmon into 12 strips. Prepare the basic recipe, topping each canapé with a twist of smoked salmon in place of the beets.

pumpernickel with sour cream & pickled herrings
Drain 12 pickled herrings. Prepare the basic recipe, topping each canapé with a pickled herring in place of the beets.

pumpernickel with sour cream & roasted bell peppers
Slice 3 bottled, roasted red bell peppers into quarters. Prepare the basic recipe using roasted peppers in place of the dressed beets.

variations

smoked mackerel pâté on finger toasts

see base recipe page 217

smoked trout pâté on finger toasts
Prepare the basic recipe, using smoked trout in place of smoked mackerel.

smoked mackerel pâté on toasted pita
Prepare the basic recipe, using pita bread instead of wholewheat bread, and slicing them across into fingers.

smoked mackerel pâté on pumpernickel squares
Prepare the basic recipe and serve with squares of pumpernickel in place of the finger toasts.

smoked mackerel pâté on french toasts
Prepare the basic recipe, using 12 thin slices of baguette in place of the wholewheat bread.

smoked mackerel pâté with cherry tomatoes
Prepare the basic recipe, spreading the pâté on the toasts and topping with halved cherry tomatoes.

crostini with blue cheese & pear

see base recipe page 218

crostini with blue cheese, pear & pecans
Prepare the basic recipe, topping each crostini with a pecan half.

crostini with blue cheese, pear & arugula
Prepare the basic recipe, topping each crostini with several arugula leaves.

crostini with blue cheese, pear & honey
Prepare the basic recipe, drizzling about 1/4 teaspoon honey over
each crostini.

crostini with blue cheese, pear & watercress
Prepare the basic recipe, topping each crostini with a sprig of watercress.

crostini with pear & pecorino
Prepare the basic recipe, using shavings of Pecorino in place of
the gorgonzola.

mouthwatering salads

Light, fresh and zingy, crisp and crunchy ... salads are the ideal way to tease the tasebuds without spoiling your appetite. Serve them before a simple supper or for a sophisticated dinner— they are perfect for both.

fennel & orange salad

see variations page 245

This light, refreshing, low-fat salad will be a hit with diners. Perfect for whetting the appetite, at the same time leaving plenty of room for the main course.

2 fennel bulbs
Juice of 1/2 lemon
3 oranges

Handful of pitted black olives
Salt and ground black pepper

Finely slice the fennel and place it in a medium bowl. Add the lemon juice and toss to combine.

Cut away the peel from the oranges. Holding the fruit over the fennel to capture the juice, cut between the membranes to remove the segments and add them to the bowl. Squeeze any juice from the membranes over the fennel before discarding the membranes.

Add the olives, season with salt and pepper, and toss to combine. Divide among four plates and serve immediately.

Serves 4

roasted bell pepper salad with mint & pumpkin seeds

see variations page 246

Roasting bell peppers brings out their sweet, intense smoky flavor. This salad is great for entertaining because it can be prepared in advance, then plated just before serving.

2 red bell peppers
2 yellow bell peppers
2 tbsp. pumpkin seeds
2 tsp. red wine vinegar

1/4 tsp. Dijon mustard
2 tbsp. olive oil
2 tsp. chopped fresh mint
Salt and ground black pepper

Preheat the oven to 450°F (230°C). Place the peppers on a baking sheet and roast for about 40 minutes, until blackened all over. Transfer to a bowl, cover with plastic wrap and leave to cool.

Meanwhile, heat a small dry frying pan, add the pumpkin seeds, and toast for 3 to 4 minutes, shaking the pan occasionally, until golden. Set aside.

In a large bowl, whisk together the vinegar, mustard, oil, and mint, and season with salt and pepper. Peel and seed the peppers, then cut the flesh into strips. Add the strips to the dressing and toss to combine. Cover and let stand for about 30 minutes. Divide the peppers among four plates, sprinkle with pumpkin seeds, and serve.

Serves 4

chargrilled zucchini salad with feta, mint & lemon

see variations page 247

The combination of sweet, smoky, and tender chargrilled zucchini, salty feta, and fresh, zingy lemon is quite divine. Make it in the summer when zucchini are in season.

1 tbsp. lemon juice
Pinch of sugar
4 tbsp. olive oil, plus extra for brushing
2 tsp. chopped fresh mint

3 zucchini
4 oz. feta cheese, crumbled
Salt and ground black pepper

Whisk together the lemon juice, sugar, olive oil, and mint. Set aside.

Preheat a griddle. Slice the zucchini on the diagonal into 1/4-inch-thick slices. Brush with oil, then place on the griddle and cook for about 4 minutes on each side, until tender and well browned or charred in placed.

Arrange the zucchini on four plates, sprinkle the feta over them, and drizzle with dressing. Season with salt and pepper to taste. Serve freshly dressed.

Serves 4

beet, halloumi & green bean salad

see variations page 248

Sweet, juicy beets; warm, salty halloumi; and crisp, fresh green beans — a fabulous combination in a simple summer salad.

1 3/4 tsp. lemon juice	Salt
1/2 tsp. grated lemon zest	1 cup (7 oz.) green beans
1/4 tsp. honey	4 cooked beets
Good pinch of dried chili flakes	9 oz. halloumi, sliced into 1/2-in. slices
2 tbsp. olive oil	

Whisk together the lemon juice and zest, honey, chili, olive oil, and a pinch of salt. Set aside.

Cook the beans for about 4 minutes in boiling water, until just tender. Drain, and refresh under cold water. Meanwhile, slice the beets, then cut the slices in the opposite direction to make matchstick strips, and place in a medium bowl. Add the beans. Drizzle the dressing over and toss to combine.

Preheat a griddle, then cook the halloumi for about 2 minutes on each side until charred. Divide the salad among four plates, top with slices of halloumi, and serve at once.

Serves 4

duck & pomegranate salad

see variations page 249

The easiest way to remove the seeds from a pomegranate is to cut the fruit in half, hold it over a bowl, and bash the back with a wooden spoon. The seeds will simply pop out.

2 duck breasts
1 tbsp. red wine vinegar
1/2 tsp. Dijon mustard
Pinch of sugar
2 tbsp. olive oil

Salt and ground black pepper
2 handfuls watercress
2 handfuls arugula
Seeds of 1 pomegranate

Score the skin on the duck in a lattice pattern and rub with salt. Heat a nonstick frying pan. Place the duck in the pan, skin side down, and cook for 10 minutes. Pour away most of the fat, turn the duck over, and cook for another 4 to 5 minutes. Transfer the duck to a board, cover with foil, and let rest.

Meanwhile, whisk together the vinegar, mustard, sugar, and olive oil, and season with salt and black pepper.

Divide the watercress and arugula leaves among four plates. Slice the duck breasts and scatter the slices over the leaves. Sprinkle with the pomegranate seeds, drizzle with dressing, and serve.

Serves 4

fig & prosciutto salad

see variations page 250

Sweet, juicy figs and salty, wafer-thin slices of prosciutto are a classic combination — and nowhere better than in this simple, luscious salad.

1 tbsp. balsamic vinegar
2 tbsp. olive oil
Salt and ground black pepper
1 scallion, finely chopped

4 handfuls mixed salad leaves (about 1/4 lb)
4 figs
8 slices prosciutto

Whisk together the vinegar and oil with salt and pepper. Divide the salad leaves among four plates. Cut the figs into wedges, and scatter them over the salads. Tear the prosciutto into bite-size pieces and scatter them on top.

Drizzle the dressing over the salads, sprinkle with scallions, and serve.

Serves 4

mango & seared beef salad with wasabi dressing

see variations page 251

Sweet, juicy mango and tender seared beef make a sublime combination in this refreshing salad. Wasabi, the pale green Japanese mustard, is very peppery (like a fiery horseradish), so add more or less according to taste.

2 sirloin steaks	Salt
3 tbsp. sunflower oil, plus extra for brushing	4 handfuls watercress (about 4 oz.)
1 tbsp. red wine vinegar	1 red onion, thinly sliced
1/2 to 1 tsp. wasabi	1 mango, peeled and pitted
Pinch of sugar	

Preheat a griddle. Brush the steaks with oil and season, then cook for 3 to 4 minutes on each side, until medium rare. Set aside.

Whisk together the oil, red wine vinegar, wasabi, and sugar, and season with salt to taste.

Put a handful of watercress on each plate, then scatter the onion over the top. Cut the mango into bite-size pieces and scatter them over the salad. Slice the steaks and divide the slices among the plates, then drizzle with the dressing and serve.

Serves 4

baby spinach, roasted squash & gorgonzola salad

see variations page 252

Roasting brings out the intense, sweet flavor of the squash, and the heat helps to melt the gorgonzola and wilt the spinach leaves to create a deliciously different salad.

1 small butternut squash
1 1/2 tbsp. olive oil, plus extra for drizzling
Salt and ground black pepper
1 tbsp. balsamic vinegar

1/2 tsp. whole-grain mustard
4 oz. baby spinach
3 1/2 oz. gorgonzola or other blue cheese, cut into slices or crumbled

Preheat the oven to 400°F (200°C). Halve, seed, and peel the squash, then slice it into twelve wedges and put in a baking dish or roasting pan. Drizzle with oil, season with salt and pepper, and toss to coat all over. Roast for about 20 minutes, until tender.

Meanwhile, whisk together the oil, vinegar, and mustard and set aside.

Divide the spinach among four plates or salad bowls and scatter the cheese over it. Add three wedges of squash to each salad, drizzle with dressing, and serve immediately.

Serves 4

avocado & grapefruit salad

see variations page 253

The combination of zingy grapefruit and creamy avocado is the perfect way to make the mouth water in anticipation of the meal to follow. This salad takes only minutes to prepare and looks stunning.

2 tsp. raspberry vinegar
1 tsp. Dijon mustard
Good pinch of sugar
1 1/2 tbsp. olive oil
Ground black pepper

4 handfuls mixed leaves, such as spinach, arugula, and watercress (about 3 oz.)
2 grapefruits (white or ruby)
2 avocados

Whisk together the vinegar, mustard, sugar, and oil, season with black pepper, and set aside.

Put the salad leaves in a large bowl. Cut away the peel from the grapefruit, then cut between the membranes to remove the segments, reserving any juice. Add the grapefruit to the salad and drizzle over the reserved juices.

Peel and pit the avocados, then cut the flesh into bite-size pieces and add them to the salad. Drizzle with the dressing, and toss to combine all the ingredients.

Arrange the salad on individual plates and serve immediately.

Serves 4

fennel & orange salad

see base recipe page 229

fennel, orange & charbroiled scallion salad
Prepare the basic recipe. Trim 2 bunches of scallions, brush with oil, then grill for 2 to 3 minutes on each side until tender. Add to the salad and serve.

fennel, orange & red onion salad
Prepare the basic recipe, adding 1/2 finely sliced red onion to the salad.

fennel & orange salad with mint
Prepare the basic recipe, sprinkling the salad with 2 teaspoons chopped fresh mint.

fennel & orange salad with chives
Prepare the basic recipe, sprinkling the salad with 1 tablespoon snipped fresh chives.

variations

roasted bell pepper salad with mint & pumpkin seeds

see base recipe page 231

roasted bell pepper & anchovy salad
Prepare the basic recipe, adding 8 anchovies, halved lengthways, to the salad.

roasted bell pepper salad with toasted pine nuts
Prepare the basic recipe, using toasted pine nuts in place of the pumpkin seeds.

roasted bell pepper & tomato salad
Prepare the basic recipe, adding 4 chopped, seeded, and peeled tomatoes to the salad.

roasted bell pepper salad with capers
Prepare the basic recipe, adding 1 teaspoon chopped, rinsed capers to the dressing. (Do not add any more salt to the dressing, as the capers are salty.)

roasted bell pepper & arugula salad
Prepare the basic recipe and serve each salad on a handful of arugula leaves.

variations

chargrilled zucchini salad with feta, mint & lemon

see base recipe page 232

chargrilled zucchini, feta & olive salad
Prepare the basic recipe, adding 4 or 5 pitted black olives to each salad.

chargrilled zucchini & pepper salad with feta
Seed two red bell peppers and cut them into eighths. Prepare the basic recipe, using 1 1/2 zucchini and broiling the pieces of pepper with the zucchini slices.

pasta salad with chargrilled zucchini & feta
Cook 4 oz. fusilli according to the instructions on the packet. Drain and set aside. Prepare the basic recipe using 2 zucchini. Toss the zucchini, feta, and dressing with the pasta and divide among four plates.

fiery chargrilled zucchini & feta salad
Prepare the basic recipe, adding 1 finely chopped, seeded fresh red chili to the dressing.

variations

beet, halloumi & green bean salad

see base recipe page 235

beet, green bean & halloumi salad with black olives
Prepare the basic recipe, tossing a handful of pitted black olives into
the salad.

beet, green bean, red onion & halloumi salad
Prepare the basic recipe, tossing 1/2 finely sliced red onion into the salad.

beet, sugar snap & halloumi salad
Prepare the basic recipe, using sugar snap peas in place of the green beans.

beet & halloumi salad with mint dressing
Prepare the basic recipe, adding 1 teaspoon chopped fresh mint to
the dressing.

beet & orange salad with halloumi
Cut away the peel from an orange, then slice between the membranes to
remove the segments. Prepare the basic recipe, adding the orange segments
to the salad.

variations

duck & pomegranate salad

see base recipe page 236

fragrant duck & pomegranate salad
Prepare the basic recipe, adding a handful of fragrant herb leaves, such as cilantro, basil, and mint, to the salad leaves.

duck, orange & pomegranate salad
Cut away the peel from an orange, then slice between the membranes to remove the segments. Prepare the basic recipe, adding the orange segments to the salad leaves.

duck & pomegranate salad with mild leaves
Prepare the basic recipe, using field greens and baby spinach leaves in place of the watercress and arugula.

duck & pomegranate salad with red onion
Prepare the basic recipe, sprinkling the salad leaves with 1/2 finely sliced red onion.

variations

fig & prosciutto salad

see base recipe page 239

nectarine & prosciutto salad
Prepare the basic recipe, using 2 pitted nectarines in place of the figs.

fig & parmesan salad
Prepare the basic recipe, scattering the salad with Parmesan shavings in place of the prosciutto.

fig & prosciutto salad with roasted chilies
Prepare the basic recipe, scattering the salads with 2 finely chopped, bottled roasted chilies.

fig & ricotta salad
Prepare the basic recipe, spooning several tablespoons of ricotta cheese over each salad in place of the prosciutto.

fig, prosciutto & watercress salad
Prepare the basic recipe, using watercress in place of the mixed salad leaves.

mango & seared beef salad with wasabi dressing

see base recipe page 240

mango & seared beef salad with cucumber
Prepare the basic recipe, tossing 1/2 small sliced cucumber into the salad with the mango and onion.

mango & seared beef salad with cilantro
Prepare the basic recipe, adding a handful of cilantro to the watercress.

kiwi & seared beef salad with wasabi dressing
Prepare the basic recipe, using 3 peeled kiwi fruit in place of the mango.

blueberry & seared beef salad with wasabi dressing
Prepare the basic recipe, using a handful of blueberries in place of the mango.

mango & chicken salad with wasabi dressing
Prepare the basic recipe, using 2 grilled chicken breasts in place of the seared steaks.

variations

baby spinach, roasted squash & gorgonzola salad

see base recipe page 243

baby spinach, new potato & gorgonzola salad
Prepare the basic recipe, using hot, freshly boiled new potatoes in place of the butternut squash.

baby spinach, roasted squash & feta salad
Prepare the basic recipe, using crumbled feta in place of the gorgonzola.

baby spinach, roasted squash & gorgonzola salad with pine nuts
Prepare the basic recipe, add 2 tablespoons toasted pine nuts over the salad.

baby spinach & gorgonzola salad with roasted beets
Prepare the basic recipe, using 3 cooked beets in place of the butternut squash. Peel the beets and cut into wedges, then drizzle with oil, season, and roast in the same way.

baby spinach & gorgonzola salad with roasted jerusalem artichokes
Prepare the basic recipe, using Jerusalem artichokes in place of the butternut squash. Scrub and peel the artichokes, then boil in lightly salted water for about 10 minutes, until almost tender. Put 1 tablespoon olive oil in a roasting pan and place in the oven for 5 minutes. Add the artichokes, toss to coat, then roast until golden.

variations

avocado & grapefruit salad

see base recipe page 244

chicken, avocado & grapefruit salad
Prepare the basic recipe, adding 2 sliced, grilled chicken breasts to the salad.

avocado, mozzarella & grapefruit salad
Prepare the basic recipe, adding four or five bocconcini (baby mozzarella) to each portion of salad.

shrimp, avocado & grapefruit salad
Prepare the basic recipe, adding 7 oz. peeled cooked shrimp to the salad.

avocado, grapefruit & scallion salad
Prepare the basic recipe, adding 1 bunch sliced scallions to the salad.

avocado, grapefruit & hazelnut salad
Prepare the basic recipe, and several tablespoons of chopped toasted hazelnuts over the top.

elegant starters

From delicious soups and tarts to irresistible shellfish and creamy pâtés that are perfect year-round, these appetizers kickstart the tastebuds and set the stage for a dramatic second act.

vichyssoise with sour cream & chives

see variations page 274

This smooth, creamy chilled soup makes an elegant appetizer for a sophisticated dinner. It's a great classic for entertaining because you can prepare it in advance.

2 tbsp. olive oil
1 onion, chopped
3 large leeks, sliced
1 potato, peeled and cut into chunks
3 cups vegetable stock

2 1/4 cups milk, plus extra if needed
2 1/4 cups light cream
Juice of 1/2 lemon, to taste
Salt and ground black pepper
Sour cream and snipped fresh chives, to garnish

Heat the oil in a deep pan, then cook the onion and leeks for about 5 minutes, until tender. Add the potatoes and stock. Bring to the boil, reduce the heat, and cover. Simmer for about 15 minutes, until the potatoes are tender.

Blend the soup until smooth in a food processor or blender. Stir in the milk, cream, and lemon juice, and season to taste. Allow to cool, then let chill for at least 2 hours.

The soup will thicken on standing, so add a splash more milk if needed before serving. Check the seasoning, squeeze in a little more lemon juice, if needed, and serve with a swirl of sour cream and a sprinkling of chives.

Serves 4

marinated seared scallops

see variations page 275

Quick and simple, yet sophisticated and utterly delicious, these scallops are the perfect way to start a dinner party. For hungry diners, add one or two extra scallops per person.

12 large scallops
1 fresh red chili, seeded and chopped
Grated zest and juice of 1 lime

2 tsp. chopped fresh mint
1 tbsp. olive oil
Salt

Put the scallops in a dish in a single layer. Whisk together the chili, lime zest and juice, mint, and olive oil with a pinch of salt. Pour over the scallops, turning to coat them evenly.

Heat a nonstick frying pan. Add the scallops and their dressing and cook for about 1 minute on each side, until just cooked through. Serve immediately, drizzled with the juices.

Serves 4

phyllo tartlets with cherry tomatoes, basil & ricotta

see variations page 276

These crisp, golden tartlets filled with baked ricotta and garlic-flavored tomatoes make an elegant start to a special meal.

8 sheets phyllo pastry
3 tbsp. butter, melted
28 cherry tomatoes
1/2 cup ricotta cheese

2 tbsp. olive oil
2 garlic cloves, crushed
Handful of fresh basil leaves
Salt and ground black pepper

Preheat the oven to 350°C (180°C). Grease a baking sheet.

Lay one sheet of phyllo pastry on a board and brush with melted butter. Lay a second sheet on top and brush with more butter. Place one-quarter of the tomatoes in the center of the phyllo. Add dollops of ricotta, nestled around and among the tomatoes. Gather the phyllo around the filling and twist the edges together to make an open tart with a firm collar around the edge. Combine the oil and garlic and drizzle this over the tomatoes and ricotta. Season with salt and pepper.

Repeat with the remaining pastry sheets and filling. Bake the tartlets on the baking sheet for 15 minutes, until crisp and golden. Serve immediately, sprinkled with fresh basil leaves.

Serves 4

roasted butternut squash soup with charbroiled chilies

see variations page 277

This sweet, fragrant, lightly spiced soup makes a wonderful appetizer — particularly in the cooler autumn and winter months, when winter squash are in season.

1 butternut squash, halved and seeded
2 tbsp. olive oil, plus extra for brushing
Salt and ground black pepper
4 mild green chilies, halved and seeded
1 onion, chopped
2 garlic cloves, chopped

1 tsp. ground cumin
1 tsp. ground coriander
1/2 tsp. ground ginger
1/4 tsp. ground cinnamon
5 cups vegetable or chicken stock
Juice of 1/2 lemon, to taste

Preheat the oven to 400°F (200°C). Brush the cut side of the squash with oil and season, then place on a baking sheet and roast for about 30 minutes, until tender. Meanwhile, preheat a griddle or broiler. Brush the chilies with oil and cook on both sides for about 4 minutes, until charred and tender. Cut into strips and set aside. In a large saucepan, fry the onion and garlic in the oil for about 5 minutes, then add the spices and stock, and bring to the boil. Reduce the heat, cover, and simmer for about 15 minutes.

Remove the squash from the oven and scoop the flesh into the soup. Process in a food processor or blender until smooth. Reheat if necessary, then squeeze in lemon juice to taste and check the seasoning. Ladle the soup into bowls and scatter strips of chilli over the top.

Serves 4

oysters with red onion, mint & cucumber vinaigrette

see variations page 278

Oysters have a salty, satisfying flavor and add a touch of panache to any meal.

1/4 red onion, finely diced
1/4 cucumber, seeded and finely diced
2 tsp. red wine vinegar
2 tbsp. olive oil

Pinch of sugar
Salt and ground black pepper
2 tsp. chopped fresh mint
12 freshly shucked oysters in the shell

Put the onion and cucumber in a small bowl and cover with the vinegar and oil. Sprinkle with the sugar and season with salt and pepper, then stir to combine. Fold in the mint and check the seasoning.

Arrange the oysters on a plate, spoon over the dressing, and serve immediately.

Serves 4

zucchini pancakes with tomato salsa

see variations page 279

These deliciously tender, creamy pancakes look stunning topped with a rich red tomato salsa. Buy a jar of salsa or make your own using the recipe on page 51.

2 zucchini, trimmed
1/4 tsp. salt
2 tbsp. self-rising flour
2 egg yolks
3 tbsp. heavy cream

2 scallions, finely sliced
1/3 cup freshly grated Parmesan cheese
Ground black pepper
Olive oil, for frying
Tomato salsa, to serve

Grate the zucchini, sprinkle with the salt, and toss to combine. Place in a colander or sieve and let drain over a bowl for 30 minutes.

Put the flour in a medium bowl. Add the egg yolks and cream, and whisk with a fork until smooth. Squeeze as much liquid out of the zucchini as possible, then add them to the batter, along with the scallions and Parmesan cheese. Season with black pepper and fold together until thoroughly combined. Heat a nonstick frying pan and add a drizzle of olive oil. Working in batches, add tablespoonfuls of the mixture to the pan, shaping them into round pancakes. Fry gently for 3 minutes on each side, until firm and golden. Keep warm while you cook the remaining mixture. Serve the pancakes warm, topped with spoonfuls of tomato salsa.

Serves 4

mussels in white wine

see variations page 280

Mussels look impressive, yet they are so easy to cook. There's something incredibly sensual about them too, and that can't help but stimulate your appetite.

2 lb. mussels, cleaned
2 tbsp. (1/4 stick) butter
2 garlic cloves, finely chopped
1/2 cup white wine

2 tbsp. heavy cream
2 tbsp. chopped fresh parsley
Salt and ground black pepper
French bread, to serve

Check the mussels and discard any that are open and do not shut when tapped. Melt the butter in a large saucepan and gently fry the garlic for about 1 minute.

Add the mussels, pour in the wine, cover the pan tightly, and cook for about 5 minutes over fairly high heat, until the mussels have opened.

Lift the mussels into four serving bowls using a slotted spoon. Discard any that have not opened. Stir the cream and parsley into the cooking liquor and season to taste. Pour the liquid over the mussels and serve with crusty French bread.

Serves 4

red onion & parmesan tartlets

see variations page 281

These simple tartlets make a stunning starter. If you want to prepare them ahead, make the custard and cut out the pastry rounds in advance, then assemble and bake the tartlets just before you want to serve them.

1/4 cup milk
1/4 cup light cream
2 garlic cloves, peeled and halved
2 red onions, cut into 6 to 8 wedges each
1 egg yolk
1/2 tbsp. all-purpose flour

1/3 cup freshly grated Parmesan cheese
9 oz. puff pastry
1 tsp. capers, rinsed
1/4 tsp. balsamic vinegar
1 tsp. olive oil
2 tsp. chopped fresh parsley

Preheat the oven to 375°F (190°C). Grease a baking sheet. In a small saucepan, bring the milk, cream, and garlic to a boil. Remove from the heat and let stand for about 15 minutes. Remove and discard the garlic. Whisk the egg yolk and flour to a smooth paste. Bring the milk and cream back to simmering, then gradually pour it into the flour mixture, whisking constantly until smooth. Return the mixture to the pan and heat gently for 4 to 5 minutes, stirring, until creamy. Remove from the heat, stir in the cheese, and season to taste. Roll out the pastry and cut out four 4 1/2-inch rounds. Lay the pastry on a baking sheet and spread the cheese custard over them, leaving a 1/4-inch border around the edge. Arrange three onion wedges on each tart, then sprinkle capers around them. Whisk together the vinegar and oil and drizzle over the onions. Bake the tarts for 15 to 20 minutes, until the pastry is crisp and golden. Serve hot, warm, or at room temperature, sprinkled with fresh parsley.

Serves 4

chicken liver pâté with garlic toasts

see variations page 282

Smooth rich chicken liver pâté is utterly irresistible and perfect for entertaining because you can make it in advance, then forget about it until you're ready to sit down to eat.

1/2 cup (1 stick) butter
2 garlic cloves, crushed
14 oz. chicken livers, trimmed and chopped
2 tbsp. brandy
1/2 tsp. fresh thyme leaves
Salt and ground black pepper

for the toasts
8 baguette slices
1 garlic clove, halved
Olive oil, for drizzling

Melt one quarter of the butter in a small nonstick pan and cook the garlic gently for 1 minute. Add the chicken livers and cook for about 5 minutes, until browned, then place them in a food processor, with all the pan juices.

Add the remaining butter, brandy, and thyme, and process until smooth. Season to taste and transfer to a bowl. Cover and chill for at least 2 hours or until firm.

To serve, toast the baguette slices on both sides until golden. Rub each slice with the cut garlic clove and drizzle with a little olive oil. Serve with the pâté.

Serves 4

roasted bell peppers with cherry tomatoes, ricotta & pesto

see variations page 283

Serve these simple roasted bell peppers with chunks of crusty white bread for mopping up the juices. For a light starter, halve the recipe and serve half a pepper per person.

2 tbsp. basil pesto
2 tbsp. olive oil
24 cherry tomatoes, halved
10 oz. jar chargrilled artichoke hearts, drained
   and cut into bite-size pieces

2 red bell peppers, halved and seeded
2 yellow bell peppers, halved and seeded
3/4 cup ricotta cheese
Ground black pepper

Preheat the oven to 400°F (200°C). Combine the pesto and olive oil, then add the tomatoes and artichokes, and fold together to coat the vegetables well.

Arrange the peppers in a baking dish large enough to hold them neatly, but not too big, and fill each with one quarter of the tomato and artichoke mixture. Add dollops of ricotta. Drizzle with any remaining oil and pesto, and add ground black pepper.

Bake for about 30 minutes, until the peppers are tender and the filling is bubbling. Serve hot or warm.

Serves 4

vichyssoise with sour cream & chives

see base recipe page 255

hot leek & potato soup
Prepare the basic recipe, but serve hot instead of chilled.

plain & simple vichyssoise with ice cubes
Prepare the basic recipe, adding a couple of ice cubes to each bowl of soup
and omitting the sour cream and chives.

vichyssoise with toasted baguette
Prepare the basic recipe. To serve, combine 4 tablespoons crème fraîche with
1 tablespooon snipped fresh chives. Halve two small baguettes and toast
them until crisp and golden. Spread with the crème fraîche mixture and
serve immediately with the soup.

vichyssoise with herbed pita toasts
Prepare the basic recipe. To serve, split 4 pita breads in half and broil on both
sides until crisp and golden. Drizzle with olive oil and sprinkle with chopped
fresh parsley and serve.

vichyssoise with red onion
Prepare the basic recipe and sprinkle the finished soup with finely diced red
onion instead of the chives.

marinated seared scallops

see base recipe page 257

marinated seared scallops with garlic
Prepare the basic recipe, adding 1 crushed garlic clove to the marinade.

marinated seared scallops with ginger
Prepare the basic recipe, adding 1 teaspoon grated fresh ginger to
the marinade.

marinated seared scallops with fresh basil
Prepare the basic recipe, sprinkling the scallops with torn fresh basil leaves
before serving.

marinated seared scallops with cilantro
Prepare the basic recipe, sprinkling the scallops with 1 tablespoon chopped
fresh cilantro before serving.

variations

phyllo tartlets with cherry tomatoes,
basil & ricotta

see base recipe page 258

phyllo tartlets with cherry tomatoes & roasted peppers
Prepare the basic recipe, adding strips of roasted pepper to the filling.

phyllo tartlets with cherry tomatoes & chives
Prepare the basic recipe, sprinkling the cooked tartlets with 1 to 2
tablespoons snipped fresh chives in place of the basil.

phyllo tartlets with cherry tomato & blue cheese
Prepare the basic recipe, using crumbled blue cheese in place of the ricotta.

phyllo tartlets with cherry tomato & goats cheese
Prepare the basic recipe, using cubed goats cheese in place of the ricotta.

phyllo tartlets with cherry tomato & arugula
Prepare the basic recipe, serving the tartlets topped with a handful of fresh
arugula leaves in place of the basil.

roasted butternut squash soup with charbroiled chilies

see base recipe page 261

roasted butternut squash soup with garlic bruschetta
Prepare the basic recipe. Toast 8 baguette slices on both sides, then rub with a cut garlic clove, drizzle with oil, and serve with the soup.

roasted butternut squash soup with sour cream
Prepare the basic recipe, adding a dollop of sour cream to each bowl of soup, and sprinkling with the chilies before serving.

roasted roasted beet soup
Prepare the basic recipe, using 3 large, peeled beets cut into wedges in place of the butternut squash.

roasted roasted pumpkin soup
Prepare the basic recipe, using a large wedge of pumpkin in place of the butternut squash.

variations

oysters with red onion, mint & cucumber vinaigrette

see base recipe page 262

oysters with shallot & tarragon vinaigrette
Prepare the basic recipe, using 1/2 finely chopped shallot in place of the red onion, and chopped fresh tarragon in place of the mint.

oysters with red onion & tomato vinaigrette
Prepare the basic recipe, using 1 finely chopped, seeded tomato in place of the cucumber.

oysters with scallion & chili vinaigrette
Prepare the basic recipe, using 2 finely chopped scallions in place of the red onion, and adding a good pinch of dried chili flakes.

oysters with red onion & green bell pepper vinaigrette
Prepare the basic recipe, using 1/2 finely diced green bell pepper in place of the cucumber.

zucchini pancakes with tomato salsa

see base recipe page 265

zucchini pancakes with sour cream & chives
Prepare the basic recipe, topping the pancakes with a dollop of sour cream and a sprinkling of snipped fresh chives instead of tomato salsa.

zucchini pancakes with sour cream & caviar
Prepare the basic recipe, topping each pancake with a dollop of sour cream and a teaspoonful of caviar.

zucchini pancakes with pesto cream
Stir 2 teaspoons pesto into 1/3 cup crème fraîche and season with black pepper. Prepare the basic recipe and top the pancakes with the pesto cream instead of salsa.

zucchini pancakes with salsa & avocado
Prepare the basic recipe, topping the pancakes with salsa and slices of ripe avocado.

zucchini pancakes with salsa & sour cream
Prepare the basic recipe and top each pancake with a spoonful of salsa and a spoonful of sour cream.

variations

mussels in white wine

see base recipe page 266

mussels in beer
Prepare the basic recipe, using a light beer in place of the wine and omitting the cream.

mussels in white wine with blue cheese
Prepare the basic recipe, using 2 finely chopped shallots in place of the garlic, and stirring 1/3 cup crumbled blue cheese into the cooking liquor in place of the cream.

mussels with sherry & chorizo
Prepare the basic recipe, adding 1 oz. finely chopped chorizo to the butter with the garlic, and using sherry in place of the white wine. Omit the cream.

mussels in white wine with garlic & chili
Prepare the basic recipe, adding 1/4 teaspoon dried chili flakes with the garlic.

red onion & parmesan tartlets

see base recipe page 269

red onion & parmesan tartlets with olives
Prepare the basic recipe, adding several pitted black olives to each tart.

red onion & parmesan tartlets with pine nuts
Prepare the basic recipe, sprinkling on 1 tablespoon pine nuts before baking the tartlets.

red onion, parmesan & prosciutto tartlets
Tear 4 wafer-thin slices of prosciutto into pieces. Prepare the basic recipe and nestle pieces of prosciutto among the wedges of onion before baking.

red onion, parmesan & chive tartlets
Prepare the basic recipe, stirring 1 tablespoon snipped fresh chives into the custard. Sprinkle with more fresh chives, instead of parsley, before serving.

variations

chicken liver pâté with garlic toasts

see base recipe page 270

duck liver pâté
Prepare the basic recipe, using duck livers in place of the chicken livers.

chicken liver pâté with sherry
Prepare the basic recipe, using sherry in place of the brandy.

chicken liver pâté with chives
Prepare the basic recipe, stirring 1 tablespoon snipped chives into the
blended pâté before chilling. Serve sprinkled with more chives.

chicken liver pâté with oregano
Prepare the basic recipe, using oregano in place of the thyme.

chicken liver pâté with toasted sourdough
Prepare the basic recipe, serving the pâté with slices of toasted sourdough
bread instead of garlic toasts.

variations

roasted bell peppers with cherry tomatoes, ricotta & pesto

see base recipe page 273

roasted bell peppers with cherry tomatoes, mascarpone & pesto
Prepare the basic recipe, using mascarpone in place of the ricotta.

roasted bell peppers with cherry tomatoes, mozzarella & pesto
Cut 5 1/2 oz. mozzarella into bite-size pieces and prepare the basic recipe using the mozzarella in place of the ricotta.

roasted bell peppers with cherry tomatoes, goats cheese & pesto
Prepare the basic recipe, using cubes of goats cheese in place of the ricotta.

roasted bell peppers with cherry tomatoes, ricotta, pesto & jalapeños
Prepare the basic recipe, adding 2 sliced, bottled jalapeños to the tomato and artichoke mixture.

index